Dear Jo

This may be a [?]
that you are allo[?]
your own trains, but I hope your
birthday is as joyous as mine was.
Thank you for everything you've done these
past months - even if it's not always
obvious, I couldn't have wished for a
better lockdown buddy.

Now, go enjoy your freedom.

with as much sentiment as I can stomach,

David.

13/07/20.

SEVENTY YEARS OF
RAILWAY
PHOTOGRAPHY

SEVENTY YEARS OF RAILWAY PHOTOGRAPHY

SEVEN DECADES BEHIND THE LENS

COLIN BOOCOCK

PEN & SWORD
TRANSPORT

First published in Great Britain in 2018 by
PEN & SWORD TRANSPORT
An imprint of
Pen & Sword Books Ltd
Yorkshire - Philadelphia

ISBN 978 1 52670 012 4

A CIP catalogue record for this book is available from the British Library

Typeset in 11/14 pt Palatino
Typeset by Aura Technology and Software Services, India
Printed and bound in India by Replika Press Pvt. Ltd.

Pen & Sword Books Ltd incorporates the Imprints of Aviation, Atlas, Family History, Fiction,
Maritime, Military, Discovery, Politics, History, Archaeology, Select, Wharncliffe Local History,
Wharncliffe True Crime, Military Classics, Wharncliffe Transport, Leo Cooper, The Praetorian
Press, Remember When, Seaforth Publishing and Frontline Publishing.

For a complete list of Pen & Sword titles please contact

PEN & SWORD BOOKS LTD
47 Church Street, Barnsley, South Yorkshire, S70 2AS, England
E-mail: enquiries@pen-and-sword.co.uk
Website: www.pen-and-sword.co.uk

Or
PEN AND SWORD BOOKS
1950 Lawrence Rd, Havertown, PA 19083, USA
E-mail: Uspen-and-sword@casematepublishers.com
Website: www.penandswordbooks.com

CONTENTS

ACKNOWLEDGMENTS

In this book, all uncredited photographs were taken by the author. In the case of photographs by others, the credit at the end of the caption shows who was the photographer, or the source of the image. In the cases of the handful of photographs in the Appendices that he has downloaded from the internet, the author has made every effort, not always with success, to trace the copyright holder where a licence does not explicitly cover copy reproduction. If he has inadvertently breached any photographer's copyright, this is not intentional; he asks any such photographer to contact him through the publisher of this book for any reproduction fee that may be due.

In some of his travels in Britain and Ireland the author has found a few of his photographs on public display without his permission, in museums, railway offices, or in two cases on major railway stations. In the case of the museums, on pointing this out to the curators, they were duly apologetic; the author was in those cases happy to grant in writing there and then his permission for the pictures' continued display without charge. He hopes he will be treated just as kindly by anyone who feels that he has similarly transgressed!

Comments in the text by the author that mention brand names for cameras, equipment, materials, mobile phones and suppliers, for example, are the author's own views based on his experience, and cannot be attributed to the publisher or its agents.

PREFACE

There are thousands of books about railways, and most are illustrated with railway photographs. So why are we launching yet another?

This book serves a modern need, I suggest, by showing how anyone interested in railways can photograph them, and can keep up-to-date throughout a long photographic career as technology improves.

The book is also a celebration. The year 2017 marks the seventieth anniversary of the year in which I took my first railway photograph, 1947. Readers can see for themselves a number of key lessons that arise from my seventy photographic years, and which hopefully I have learned. The quality of pictures from a Brownie Box camera cannot compare with that from modern digital cameras, and now even mobile phones, and there is a whole gamut of camera types, film sizes, and means of presenting results through printing, projection and the internet that can be studied.

There are two key aspects to the photographs and text in this book. Firstly, readers are invited to enjoy with me the fun of looking through pictures of our favourite means of transport, pictures that show how railways have changed over seventy years. I think they have improved substantially, but not every enthusiast agrees with me! We can also see a little of how overseas railways look different from our own, and how they respond to different conditions of climate, topography, economics and geography, different, that is, from the United Kingdom.

Secondly, Appendices 1 and 2 tackle some of the detailed technical aspects of railway photography, both using traditional films, and modern digital methods. These appendices draw on my experience over the years. I did my own black-and-white processing in the days when film was the dominant form of photography. I prepare my own material for publication in this digital age using my computer and equipment connected to it.

Appendix 3 is aimed at camera technique, and in particular getting the composition of a photograph right at that stage. I advocate a number of simple rules, which I learned from various sources from school art lessons and from other, more experienced photographers. I also break all of these rules in a lot of the pictures in this book, for which I claim to have valid reasons. The challenge is for readers to recognise which rules are broken in which photographs!

Appendix 4 looks at what we can do to make sure our photograph collections can be used after we have died, to avoid them being consigned to a skip.

In the end, however, whatever stand one takes as to what is the best camera to use, how pictures should be composed, whether to project from slides or digital media, whether to use colour or monochrome, and how to store and access the thousands of photographs one amasses in a lifetime, the nub of the matter comes down to the imagination and skill of the individual photographer. Despite what I wrote in the second paragraph of this Preface, a good photographer can get surprisingly good results from modest equipment. See what you think when you look through the pictures that follow in this book. With all the upgrading, technical advances, new materials and decades of experience, has there been a significant improvement in my photography from the 1950s to the 2010s?

You decide.

INTRODUCTION

When I was about three years old, according to my mother, she drew me a picture of a railway engine on our blackboard at home. She said that I promptly corrected it!

I cannot remember any time in my life when railways have not been a key element in my interests outside my school, family and friends. When I was a small boy, I was fascinated when we saw four-coach green suburban electric trains passing over the level crossing at our local station at Addlestone in Surrey. Even the big wooden crossing gates held me enthralled – they opened and closed when the nearby signalman turned a large wooden wheel, and locked into position with a clatter when steel clamps emerged from the road surface.

My pocket money served to buy sweets and railway booklets. These included Ian Allan's pocketbook series entitled *My Best Railway Photographs*, with pictures taken by the leading railway photographers of the 1940s. Photographs of steam locomotives, express and local trains taken by O.J. Morris, Canon Eric Treacy, C.R.L. Coles, C.C.B. Herbert and M.W. Earley caught my imagination. Some of the pictures of the ancient and wonderfully weird railways and locomotives that were sought out for the camera of H.C. Casserley I can remember to this day. And the photographs by R.W. Kidner of massive American steam trains made me realise that there was much more to railways than just those we could find in the UK.

In summer 1947, when I was nine years old, I suddenly realised that, like these well-known men, I could take pictures of trains if I had a camera. I persuaded my father to take me down to our nearest station, at that time Bournemouth Central, with his Nagel folding camera loaded with a 120-size film. With his guidance, and with Dad setting the camera, I took three photographs that day. Dad took one which was undoubtedly better than mine, but the seed was sown. Four photographs, remember, used up half a film when the negative size was 2¼ inches by 3¼ inches.

For Christmas 1949, I received a Brownie box camera, and spent two days and two films on the former Lancashire & Yorkshire Railway station at Colne, the east-Lancashire town where my grandparents lived. A dull December day in the industrial north of England was not ideal for a fixed-exposure camera, but two of the pictures were in a brief sunny spell and were okay. I was learning.

My box camera went with me whenever I travelled, usually by bicycle, to places within reach of Bournemouth such as Salisbury or Eastleigh. I had joined the Bournemouth Junior Railway Club when I was ten; I am still a member though we discarded the word 'Junior' in 1953 when we thought we were all grown up. I began to get some acceptable photographs once I realised the limitations of the basic box camera and kept within them.

On seeing the improvement in my photography, my parents decided that I could borrow on permanent loan my father's Nagel folding camera. I got several pretty poor results in 1953, but I advanced thereafter into producing some good photographs that are eminently reproducible today. One of these was the first of my photographs to be published, a scene at Bournemouth Central after two locomotives had collided in January 1955 which appeared in the *Railway Magazine*;

at that time the magazine did not pay reproduction fees, relying on the fact that people liked to see their pictures in print, rather like they do on the internet today!

In 1956, by which time I was earning a moderate wage in my engineering apprenticeship at Eastleigh Locomotive Works, I bought a second-hand Zeiss Super-Ikonta camera which took eleven 2¼ inch square pictures on a 120 film. The quality of negatives that emerged from this camera was excellent and set the level of quality that I have aspired to ever since.

By this time, I was developing and printing my own pictures. My darkroom was my bedroom, the window blocked as required by a large board so as to keep out the light. Three decades later my darkroom went up into the loft.

In 1958, I was printing some pictures I had taken on the Railway Correspondence & Travel Society's tour to Austria when it dawned on me that scenes in the Alps shown in black-and-white did not have the impact of the magnificent scenery I had seen with my naked eye. So, in spring 1959, I bought my first colour camera, a brand new Voigtländer Vito IIa folding 35mm camera with a lens designed for good colour integrity, and filled it with Agfa CT18 colour slide film. A necessary addition was a Weston Master III exposure meter so that I could ensure the slides were correctly exposed. They all were. I can still get big enlargements off the first film I put through that camera. I liked the Vito IIa so much that I did not replace it until 1987, twenty-eight years later!

Liking the convenience and lighter weight of 35mm, I traded in my Super-Ikonta in 1962 for a Periflex 3. Using Ilford Pan F black-and-white film some results were as good as the larger format had produced. Others were less so as the camera developed a couple of faults including the two halves of its focal-plane shutter sometimes catching each other up and blanking off part of the image! This camera's replacement in 1970 was a second-hand Rollei 35, a compact German-made 35mm camera that fitted in a pocket and produced excellent results.

By this time, the only active steam locomotives working in the UK were in industry, most particularly the coal industry. Then living in South Wales, I had plenty of scope for photography in the coalfields, as again I did when we moved to Doncaster in 1971, and then to Glasgow in 1976. In parallel I was assiduously photographing the modern railway scene.

A decade later, I equipped myself with two Minolta single-lens reflex cameras, which gave me total satisfaction for quality of colour and black-and-white images. By this time, there was some steam working of special trains on BR, and plenty of activity on the growing selection of preserved railways around the country.

From 1956, I toured abroad when I could afford to, with a gap in the mid-1970s until our children were old enough to enjoy it. Retirement in 1996 gave me more time for world travel. With my wife Mary, I ventured to other continents such as Africa, America and Asia. Some charity work in the 1990s led us to eastern Europe, from where we have gained some very good friends and some exciting travel destinations including Istanbul.

The maddest thing Mary and I did was to travel round the world by train – wherever there were railways to travel on – in 2004. This was my first digital photography tour, in which I learned a lot of lessons, like never take a new camera on holiday with you! But we persevered, and neither of us has used any film since that year. Digital photography has been the way forward since before the start of the twenty-first century. The consistency of photograph quality that I now have, coupled with the incredible facilities in modern software for bringing out the best in photographic images, in my opinion make digital photography the only sensible method now available.

Railway photography divides into at least seven different types:

Record photography, including accurate studies of standing locomotives or rolling stock, showing as much detail as possible; or studies of railway infrastructure such as stations, signalboxes and yards.

I tried to take a good photograph of every British Railways class and major variant of locomotive, not fully succeeding as distant classes were scrapped before I got to them. My definitive collection of locomotive studies is in black-and-white, and has enabled me to illustrate three books under the *Locomotive Compendium* genre, one each on the Southern Region of BR, Irish locomotives and diesel multiple units in the British Isles. The key to a good record photograph is sharpness, good lighting – not necessarily sunny which can produce shadows that hide detail – a fine grain image and an angle of approach of a quarter to three-quarters front view, though a side view can show locomotive proportions well, too.

Because railway stations and other buildings are often of considerable architectural merit, these can be sensible subjects for a railway photographer. It is a different field from record photography of trains because, for one thing, buildings are so much bigger than trains and the photographer often has little space in which to compose the picture he or she wants; it is not always possible to stand back far enough to get the ideal view. I find that a wide-angle lens is ideal for many shots of large buildings, but the looming hazard is perspective distortion. I abhor converging verticals in pictures of buildings, so the camera position needs to be chosen wisely. A friend of mine has a perspective-correcting additional lens that he fits in front of his camera lens, and this seems to be a practical way of modifying perspective in colour slide photography. Digital printing using image adjustment software can correct converging verticals easily, as described in Appendix 2 of this book.

Record photographs in colour need also to have accurate rendering of the

A record photograph needs to show all available detail clearly, but need not exclude nice things like clouds and some of the surroundings. This portrait of BR standard Class 4 2-6-4T 80035 at Willesden is one of my better record shots.

livery colour of the subject. It is surprising how widely the colours of BR dark green and rail blue can vary depending on the film used, the value of light available, and the camera lens used; and that presupposes no further changes during the printing or Photoshop processes!

Action photography, the one that impresses many observers, for example showing trains moving at speed or steam locomotives working hard with billowing exhausts.

This is a potential book subject of itself! One key specialist feature is the need normally to prevent any sign of movement in the picture. A fast shutter speed is one requirement, but the angle of view is also relevant. A train that is almost head-on will reveal much less

movement to the camera than one passing and viewed from the side. Most lineside photographers will opt for a three-quarters or seven-eighths front view, partly because most lineside photographic positions dictate that that is the most practical angle. A very fast shutter speed such as 1/1000th second or faster usually requires the lens iris to be wide open; this reduces significantly the depth of focus, so it is more difficult to render the front and the back of the train sharply enough. A compromise has to be made. I follow the advice of O.J. Morris who said that one should focus on the front third of the train and stop down enough to get the engine front sharp. If one focuses directly on the front of the engine with a film camera, the bulk of the train behind it will often be unsharp, something I learned from early experience. With digital cameras and mobile phone cameras, their inherent longer depth of focus enables me to focus on the first vehicle of a train, knowing that the rest will be satisfactorily sharp.

If light levels are low, such as in London Underground stations, to get a

Steam locomotives have the whip hand when it comes to action photographs simply because of their exhausts. It helps if the scenery is bordering on the spectacular, too! This is the Kaaiman's River bridge in South Africa's Western Cape, seen as the morning mist off the Indian Ocean begins to lift. Class 19D 4-8-2s 2749 and 3324 cross the bridge hauling the heavy tour train comprised of the 'Union Limited' stock, examples of the pre-war 'Blue Train' vehicles. Action photographs are usually best where a train is not moving especially fast.

good exposure may force a slower shutter speed than one would want. When I was using 400ASA film, nowadays known as ISO400, I settled on a shutter speed of 1/60th second with the lens at full aperture. Any train movement had to be as near head-on as possible, so I tended to fire the shutter when the train had emerged from the tunnel but was not too close, the picture being made more interesting by the presence of people on the platform.

A different form of action photography takes a side-on picture of a passing locomotive, with the camera following the engine in the viewfinder very closely. Experts in this technique, which is called 'panning', say they use a relatively slow shutter speed, say 1/25th second or slower, and are happy that the background and foreground are very blurred as are any moving parts on the locomotive. It is difficult to get a sharp image of the bulk of the locomotive with this method, but experience leads to expertise and the result can be a stunning portrayal of a locomotive at speed. This is not one of my skills.

Illustrative photography, photographs with a specific aim to back up an article or descriptive text, for example details of traction and rolling stock livery variations.

There are one or two of these in this book. I remember taking a group of pictures of features of the Liverpool Overhead Railway in 1955 to illustrate my very first published article which was for the magazine *Trains Illustrated*. Rather than just take pictures of trains, which is what I had normally done until then, I widened my scope to take in such things

This example of illustrative photography shows the livery on the side of a Class 170 'Turbo-Star' diesel multiple unit that displayed the first new colours of the Anglia franchised operator. This was an early use of vinyls to put more complicated liveries on trains. This scene was at Norwich station. This type of photography serves a distinct purpose, in this case to illustrate a book on train liveries.

as a big lift bridge near a dock – waiting until a train went over the bridge, of course! – and a general view of the area around Herculaneum Dock station (see picture in Chapter 2).

More recently, I illustrated articles by visiting depots and works to show rolling stock under various forms of repair, with some detailed shots showing lifting, or a wheel profiler at work, or spray painting going on. My article in the former magazine *Entrain* about maintenance of axle bearings had me visiting Warrington and taking pictures of the different types of wagon suspensions and axle ends on view there, something I would never have done without the specific need to illustrate the article.

Artistic photography, something most of us aim at though we usually fall short in achieving.

We make a picture out of a scene by dint of careful composition, framed by objects in the scene; trees, posts, a bridge or buildings, say. A photographer can make use of *contre-jour* lighting, silhouettes, and so forth. This is the most individualistic branch of railway photography. People like Colin Gifford and Colin Garratt have very distinctive forms of artistic expression of railways through the camera. The latter takes enormous effort in setting up a scene, even once declaring that he had bought some particular clothes for an Indian boy so that they matched the colours of a locomotive he would pose near. Others make their pictures from whatever scene is in front of them, often looking at them from completely unusual angles.

Artistic photography is so individual, it would be wrong of me to impress any particular style on readers. The only advice I would give is that, other things being equal - which they are not always – it is good to place the main subject on 'the intersection of two

thirds'. Mentally divide the scene up into three divisions both horizontally and vertically, have the main subject, for example, the front of the locomotive, in one or other of the points where the 'third' lines cross, and you do not go far wrong. You will quickly see in this book that I don't always obey this rule, though I do have my reasons. So, go out there, and express yourselves!

Detail photography, picking out small details such as a shedplate, a nameplate, cylinder drain cocks, axle bearings – you name it, the scope is endless.

I have already referred to this when writing about wagon bearings above. It's a form of record photography and is used for several purposes. In some cases, it can be to illustrate some written work. In others, it may be to help a modeller make his model correctly when a general picture of the locomotive or carriage, for example, doesn't show up enough detail. My picture of the inside of an A4 corridor tender in Chapter 8, can be used as an example, though that was not its original purpose.

Railway people photography, railwaymen or women at work, passengers rushing to catch a train or milling around, an engine driver in full concentration; again, the scope is very wide.

Sometimes you will need the person's permission to take a picture of them at work, particularly if you intend it to be published, though it is rarely refused. A group of passengers on a platform is less personal, though watch them carefully for they don't always stand where you want them to – a key problem is the person at the back of the platform who moves forward in front of you just as his or her train comes in; this is one hazard you can do nothing about, if you are of a polite disposition.

One person's view of what is artistic is not necessarily another's. I saw this very relaxed dog watching the frantic rushing about of station staff at Sargan Vitesi in Serbia on 30 April 2010 as they tried to cajole railtour passengers to rejoin their 760mm gauge train. The Class 83 0-8-2 is out of sight behind a post, but it does not matter – the subject is the event, not the train as such. The picture is framed by the tree above and the furniture on the extreme right. The dog and the frame lead the eye to the anxious railway staff.

Detail photography can take many forms. This one shows part of the valve gear and one crosshead on Deutsche Reichsbahn [DR] 2-10-0 freight engine 50.001 in the Technical Museum in Berlin. This is the only railway picture in this book that required the use of flash to get sufficient light. The flash was almost too bright.

Model railway photography, a specialist branch that required its own photographic techniques.

Because models are small, to get any depth of focus with a conventional camera it is essential to stop down to something like f/22. In anything less than bright sunshine, a tripod is ideal so that a slow shutter speed can be used. For this, any model trains must stop running, because movement will be blurred. How different this is with mobile phone cameras; I cover this in more detail in Chapter 8.

One problem that model railway photographers face is how to eliminate unwanted background detail. A general view across a very realistic model railway quite often picks up images of people milling around in the distance, towering above the models, or just the rest of the room where the details are quite wrong for the composition required. I often resort to blanking out such extraneous detail using Adobe Photoshop Elements. This can be by painting out the background, or by copying nearby detail and pasting something more relevant over the offending area.

Portraits of model items, such as the model Midland compound I illustrate in Chapter 8, offer a further challenge. In the caption, I describe how I used sheets of white A3 paper to cover all foreground and background detail so that the model stood out. A clear white background was a requirement of the magazine for which the photograph was taken.

Readers will have twigged that several of these types of railway photography overlap. An action picture can be pictorial. Detail photography usually is also record photography. People appear in various other types of railway pictures. So, the borderlines are blurred. The rules

RIGHT: Railway people at work often make interesting pictures. These two are refitting the headlamp on a Class SY 2-8-2 in the depot at Jalainur, northern China, seen during a tour of mines and steelworks systems in 2004. This picture demands the title, quoting from Confucius, 'Many hands make light work.'

BELOW: Model railways are quite difficult to photograph because their small size forces the camera to get close to the subject. This substantially reduces the depth of focus available. With a normal camera, it is necessary usually to mount the camera on a tripod or other firm surface and stop down to f/22 or smaller, using a long exposure. Using flash seems often to result in very uneven lighting of the model subject area, so I do not. In modern times life is so much easier; the mobile phone camera with which this photograph was taken in 2016 has a much longer depth of focus because the lens is so small. The ability of mobile phone cameras to set the exposure automatically, and get it right nearly every time, makes them ideal for photographing model railways, so long as the degree of enlargement needed is not huge. This 0-gauge cameo layout illustrates a small yard shunted by an early 0-6-0ST locomotive of the London & South Western Railway, and belongs to a trustee of the Famous Trains model railway in Derby. The layout is sometimes exhibited there.

of good composition can apply to all types of railway photography, however. See Appendix 3.

The digital revolution

I cover digital railway photography in some detail in Appendix 2, as well as referring to some of its features in the later chapters. Suffice it for me to say here that I am completely sold on digital photography as the way forward for me. Its advantages outweigh its minor disadvantages. Digital photography has reached the stage that one can produce affordable high quality photographs digitally. My own results are sharper, have more consistent colours, do not deteriorate over time, and can be duplicated and stored so one need not damage or lose original negatives or slides. And if you have a film developed and printed commercially nowadays, the processor will print them digitally.

I give 'slide shows' to railway enthusiast groups and others as a way of promoting the charity Railway Children, and can carry all my twenty-odd illustrated shows on a small memory stick. I cannot drop a cassette full of slides on the floor, nor accidentally project any upside-down, as has

This is the earliest known photograph that links the author with railways. Six-year-old Colin Boocock poses very seriously alongside the Chessington Zoo miniature railway 4-4-0 *Princess Elizabeth* in the summer of 1944. The locomotive had an internal combustion engine fuelled by gas; liquid fuel was in short supply. The cabside inscription optimistically reads 'Speed ..... 80 M.P.H.' Surely only the British would run miniature railways when there was a war on? (*Sidney Boocock*)

During a delightful tour of Sardinia in 2002, run by the Railway Touring Company, I am standing on the front of SLM-built 2-6-0T *Gioto* with my trusty Minolta X-300 camera loaded with Fuji Reala 100 colour negative film. This neat 950mm gauge engine gamefully hauled our charter train from Sorgorno to Mandas. A popular feature of the tour was *al fresco* lunches at remote locations while our steam train rested alongside us. Sublime!
(*Mrs Mary Boocock, scanned from print*)

happened when using 35mm slides. And I have a solid back-up on my lap-top computer as well as the computer itself being backed up regularly on an external hard drive.

Interestingly, as I write this there are signs of a small rebound with some photographers wanting to move forward with film photography, and at least one manufacturer who abandoned films is thinking of supplying the market again. This is rather akin to the upsurge in 2016 of the popularity of vinyl records, and for much the same reasons. Some people hold that the sound from vinyl records is purer than can be achieved by the digital sound systems we hear every day.

Equally, there are those photographers who tell me that a good colour slide cannot be beaten in quality by a digital image. The one area I will give ground in is that the digital projectors we use for shows and lectures cannot yet project such high quality images as the top quality slide projectors can. Most have a picture width of 1,024 pixels, and the best are not reaching 2,000, whereas good digital photographs can be ten times as wide than the means to project them, and can make prints that match the best from films.

The watchword with digital photography is: 'Watch this space!'

CHAPTER 1

THE 1940S – BEGINNINGS

As a boy, I enjoyed buying the small booklets that Ian Allan Ltd. produced under the generic title *My Best Railway Photographs*. These were small, landscape format paperbacks with one black-and-white picture on each main page and informative captions. They gave me the idea that anyone with a camera could take photographs of trains. Until then I had never been allowed to hold my father's folding camera, a Nagel Librette dating from the 1928 to 1931 period. This used size 120 film, eight negatives to a roll.

I must have been quite persuasive, because one sunny Sunday afternoon in 1947 my father took me to our local station, Bournemouth Central. We first walked on to the Up platform, where a train had backed in from the sidings, propelled in by 'King Arthur' class 4-6-0 792 *Sir Hervis de Revel*. This locomotive thus became the subject of my first ever photograph. Only twenty years later did I realise that it was something of a scoop. This engine was the only 'Scotch Arthur' to have been fitted with a Lemâitre five-jet blastpipe and wide chimney, which it lost five years later in 1952. We then went through the subway to the Down platform from where there was a better view of almost everything, and each of us photographed the train engine, 789 *Sir Guy*, glorious in clean malachite green. Then at the western end of the station I took one of the station shunting engine Class M7 0-4-4T 112. That had used up half the roll of film, so we called it a day. When the small contact prints came back from the shop, I was hooked.

At a time when wages and salaries were low, photography was seen as an expensive hobby. With only eight pictures on a film, people were careful not to waste money on frivolous or potentially unsuccessful photographs. We had no aids to judge the correct exposures, and many of the photographs we took around that time were significantly over-exposed, leading to dense negatives and grainy enlargements, if we could afford them, which we usually could not. At the end of a film, the backing paper had to be taped down to prevent light getting in round the edges. The roll would be presented at the local chemist or photographic shop for developing and contact printing, and a week to ten days later we would go back to the shop to collect the prints. All eight would be scrutinised closely, and usually treasured, put in albums or otherwise stored.

I started off by putting mine in large albums, using corner pieces to hold the small prints in place, four to a page. Luckily, I was fastidious enough to mark film and negative numbers next to the prints, and short captions showing where they were taken and usually the dates. After all these decades, I still have these first albums and I am thankful that I did that. Even today I can lay my hands on my early photographs and the associated negatives in less than five minutes if I need to. It makes producing a book such as this much less of a chore. I just wish I had been as sensible and had catalogued my colour slides in later decades! But family life took precedence in allocating my time, and sometimes now I struggle to find a slide that I know I took, say, in the 1970s, in less than twenty minutes. And I am often finding slides I had forgotten I had taken. There is a lesson here for all aspiring photographers.

In 1946, we made the long journey by train from Bournemouth West to Colne in east Lancashire to visit my grandparents. I was so used to seeing Southern locomotives around Bournemouth that I recall being astonished to see an LMS engine at the front of our train, the 9:45am 'Pines Express' to Manchester. It was a dirty black Stanier Class 5, carrying the number 5056. The carriages were all LMS main line corridor coaches. The seats in the compartments were dusty – if you smacked the cushions a pall of dust arose, mainly soot and coal dust. In those days one did not wear best clothes for train travel! I took a couple of photographs with my father's camera while we waited for our connecting train at Manchester Victoria, and another at Colne when we were on our way back. But I had to wait until I had my own camera before I could really start out on a career of railway photography.

My early enthusiast years, like many other people's I guess, included several missed opportunities. I did not know about the 1948 locomotive exchanges until after they had happened. I first read about them in *Trains Illustrated*, and realised that those trains worked by 'foreign' engines on the London Waterloo to Exeter run had called at Salisbury which was just thirty-one miles from where we lived, an easy journey on a Hants & Dorset bus. We didn't have the benefit of modern communications such as the internet to keep abreast of events. So I missed seeing an A4 or a 'Duchess' at Salisbury, or an LNER Class O1 2-8-0 at Eastleigh.

There were family excursions on which I was able to take the odd photograph. In 1948, we went for a week at the Butlin's holiday camp at Penychain, just outside Pwllheli

in North Wales. I can remember the journey there to this day. From Paddington, I sat at the right hand side of the compartment watching for passing trains. Much to my astonishment we passed two LNER trains within the first hour of the trip – as a mere ten-year-old I was ignorant of the loop off the Great Central route at this point. I saw WD 2-8-0s with numbers in the 90000 series, not as in my Ian Allan *ABC* which showed them as in the 77000 series. We reversed at Ruabon and traversed the Cambrian route through Llangollen and Oswestry, past Bala Lake, where we saw a narrow gauge industrial engine, and on round the coast after Barmouth Junction. I spent a lot of that week sitting on Penychain station watching the trains, most of which were worked by the outside-framed 'Dukedog' 4-4-0s. The most modern trains in the area were the LMS ones with Ivatt 2-6-2Ts that terminated at the small junction station nearby at Afon Wen that we could see in the near distance from the rocky beach. My father took me on that train to Carnarvon, as the English spelled it then, to catch a bus to Llanberis, where we caught a train up the Snowdon Mountain Railway. Unlike today, there was no queue for seats! I took a couple of photographs on the mountain, but no pictures of the Cambrian 0-6-0s I saw on the way from and to London, nor of the 'Dukedogs' I saw every day passing the camp. It just never occurred to me that that would have been a sensible thing to do. So I have no record of those scenes. It took me a long time to learn that lesson.

We went to another holiday camp in summer 1949, the second and last attempt at such a holiday. This was in Hayling Island. With my father keeping up with me, I managed to walk across the island from the camp to the railway station. A diminutive 'Terrier' 0-6-0T was working the branch train from Havant, and with my father's help I took its photograph.

The 1940s concluded with a major step forward for me. For Christmas 1949, I was given a Brownie box camera. East Lancashire in late December didn't have the light that best suited a box camera; it was a particularly dull week. My photographs taken during a couple of days at Colne station were dire; I took several photographs that did not include all of the subject, and most were significantly underexposed. Nowadays the images on such thin negatives can often be rescued by programs such as Adobe Photoshop, but using the printing technology of the 1940s/1950s the contact prints just came out grey. The weak sun did shine for a Stanier Class 5, and for a

4F on a Skipton train, which gave me the knowledge that I could get acceptable pictures so long as I waited for the sun. Again, I was learning. Fortunately, later in the 1950s I was able to get good photographs of all the locomotive classes I had seen in Colne that December – former Lancashire & Yorkshire Railway 2-4-2Ts, Stanier 2-6-4Ts, Midland compounds and 2Ps, and a couple of Hughes 'Crab' 2-6-0s.

But the whole of the UK's railways were out there – waiting!

Nagel Librette folding camera, 3¼in x 2¼in – mostly under parental guidance.
My first railway photograph was this one, of 792 *Sir Hervis de Revel* at Bournemouth Central on a Sunday afternoon in 1947 after backing some stock into the Up platform for the next train to London Waterloo. It was taken under my father's guidance using his Nagel Librette camera. I used the camera's prism viewfinder, into which I had to look downwards to view a small reverse image of the subject.

Across on the Down platform, my father and I both photographed *Sir Guy* standing ready for departure for London. This was my father's version, in which he used a piece of yellow gelatine foil covering the lens as a filter to darken the sky's blue tones. My unfiltered version was less striking, and omitted most of the train and thus had far less impact. I learned about composition rules in later years. (*Sidney Boocock*)

Also on my first afternoon of railway photography, I took this study of the station shunting engine, M7 0-4-4T 112. From the western extension of Bournemouth Central's Down platform, we had a superb view of all train and locomotive movements. This end of the platform, Britain's second longest after Manchester Victoria/Exchange, was opposite the full length of the locomotive depot. 112's main duties were to haul the Bournemouth West portion of any multi-part train bound for London out from the station into the siding alongside the depot, and then propel the coaches complete with passengers to the back of the then-arrived portion from Weymouth, an operation not always successfully completed if the buck-eye couplings did not fully engage at first impact. Sometimes two or three attempts had to be made, the connection being made with an ever-louder clang that echoed round the station roof!

A disadvantage in keeping a film set of unprotected negatives in their original brown envelope was that they could occasionally be damaged by careless extraction from among their neighbouring negatives. My photograph of the LMS Class 5 at the head of the 'Pines Express' at Bournemouth West was one such. We were on our way to the north to visit my grandparents in summer 1947. The engine on this occasion was 4826. I have attempted, not fully successfully, to repair the image using Photoshop Elements. The steam escaping from the injector pipe is not genuine, but covers up a seriously scratched area.

At the end of the holiday, while we waited for the stock for the morning through train to London Euston to be placed in Colne station, I was able to get this picture of a Fowler Class 4 2-6-4T waiting in the Down bay platform. Presumably, it was ready to move off with a train bound for Skipton or Leeds, a journey that is not possible by rail now.

On our journeys to visit grandparents, we had to change stations in Manchester; the 'Pines Express' from Bournemouth arrived at London Road or Mayfield but services to Colne departed from Victoria which meant a taxi ride between them. I took the opportunity on our outward journey in 1947 to photograph a former Lancashire & Yorkshire Railway 0-6-0 at Victoria. It was so dirty we cannot see on the photograph where the engine number was, let alone read it! My youthful inexperience caused me not to notice the presence of the lamppost until it was partly obscuring the engine. The post is in fact the clearest image in the picture – everything behind it is affected by the pervading fug in the northern industrial atmosphere. Nothing can brighten up this image of a dirty locomotive in dismal surroundings.

Our holiday camp visit in North Wales in 1948 was an eye-opener. We even had a trip up Snowdon on the mountain railway. I was allowed to take this photograph of rack engine No. 6 *Padarn* waiting to descend from the summit to Llanberis. The other engine in the picture is No. 5 *Moel Siabod*.

On another visit to Bournemouth Central in 1948, I was interested to see small 0-4-0T 99, of the former London & South Western Railway's B4 class, waddling around the locomotive depot. Its duties included shunting the coal wagons near the coaling crane, and moving dead locomotives around the shed yard. Close scrutiny of the photograph shows the words NO BRAKE chalked on the cabside. The mind boggles!

In summer 1948, my parents and I stayed for a few days with my mother's friend in Cambridge. I spent some time on the station, my first venture alone with my father's camera! This apple-green B1 4-6-0 caught my attention with BRITISH RAILWAYS in Gill Sans on the tender and large cabside numbers 61334. Yet the livery was otherwise still the former LNER style and layout with black-and-white lining and it had yet to receive a smokebox-door numberplate. BR was to decide on its corporate liveries the following year, so the pre-nationalisation colours held sway during the interim period in which most locomotives received their new running numbers.

The next summer, 1949, my father and I walked from our holiday camp to Hayling Island station. When we got there, the diminutive train engine, A1X 0-6-0T 2659, had run round its three-carriage train and was ready to leave for Havant. Only a few months later, these sweet little Stroudley-designed machines would begin to be turned out from works in BR's lined black livery, which suited them far better than the Southern Railway wartime plain black.

Brownie box camera, 3¼in x 2¼in

If I am honest, the first two films I put through the box camera that I received for Christmas 1949 were a near disaster in the very dull December light! However, the sun did shine for this view of LMS 4F 0-6-0 No. 44486 carrying an Accrington shed plate, 24A. The locomotive was about to leave Colne with a stopping train for Skipton, a short section of line that was closed in the early 1960s. The low viewpoint comes from the facts that (a) I was only eleven years old, (b) not tall, and (c) I had to look down into the viewfinder which was recessed into the top of the camera. Nonetheless, I thought the result was encouraging. It did teach me that using the camera within its limitations would bring better photographs.

CHAPTER 2

THE 1950S – STEAM'S POST-WAR HEYDAY

The years of my teens were also the years when I became established as a railway photographer. My first published photograph, of a train crash at Bournemouth Central, appeared in the *Railway Magazine* in 1955. My first published writing was an article about the Liverpool Overhead Railway which appeared in *Trains Illustrated* magazine in 1956.

To get that far had taken eight or nine years from when I started taking railway photographs at the age of nine. At the time progress seemed slow. Looking back, I am delighted how fast I moved from slightly fuzzy box camera images to pin sharp and well-composed railway pictures in less than a decade.

My father taught me how to make contact prints, in a dark space under our kitchen sink. I began to get sharper and more contrasty images that way than the local shops produced using their print machines. Even so, the normal print size was 3¼ inches by 2¼ inches, the same size as the negatives. If I wanted anything bigger, such as postcard size, I had to pay a professional shop to make enlargements.

In 1953, my parents were becoming more complimentary about the photographs I was achieving with my box camera, and decided to let me borrow my father's Nagel Librette folding camera on permanent loan. This camera dated from around 1928-31. It had a good lens, a Compur shutter and a small prism viewfinder that reversed the tiny image the photographer could see when looking down into it. I discovered that the camera also had a wire frame viewfinder which, when raised into position, enabled the photographer to look through the eyepiece directly at the subject with no intervening glass, the wire frame giving a very good guide as to the content of the image. I tried that from the start, and found it very easy to use. I also bought a cheap plastic exposure calculator that I could set for the film speed, the time of day, the type of light – bright sun, hazy sun, cloudy bright, cloudy dull, etc. – and the type of subject, landscape, close-up for example. While this was crude, it was better than complete guesswork, and enabled me to set a shutter speed and lens aperture suitable for the photograph being taken. Most black-and-white films had enough exposure latitude to cope with the variations in negative density that came from using this aid.

The exposure calculator did not tell me what shutter speed to use, of course. I had to find this out by experience. I soon realised that a fast-moving train could only just be stopped with the Nagel camera's fastest shutter speed of 1/250th second. I also soon adopted the policy of using 1/100th second for still photographs to avoid any sign of camera shake, so long as there was enough light to enable the lens to be stopped down to f/6.3 or smaller to give me enough depth of focus. Otherwise, if the light was really low, I would use a slower shutter speed and hold my breath! Thankfully, most of the moving trains I photographed were at relatively slow speeds. A steam locomotive working hard at slow speed looks considerably more impressive visually than one flying past with little exhaust to show. I had to wait until the 1980s before I had a camera with a shutter that would manage 1/1000th second shutter speed reliably.

When I had enough money, later during my engineering apprenticeship at Eastleigh Locomotive Works, I bought an enlarger with a decent Wray Supar lens, a red safelight to be able to see in a blacked-out darkroom, an open adjustable frame that could hold printing papers up to 10in x 8in, some trays for holding the liquids, and bottles of the basic chemicals, developer and fixer. My father and I made up a board that fitted tight within my bedroom window space, thus blacking out the room. By summer 1956, I was producing satisfactory postcard prints of all my photographs with remarkably little wastage. I joined the Eastleigh & District Photographic Society, took part in their competitions with some larger sized railway pictures, and was commended for one or two of them.

One of my aims became to take at least one good photograph of every type of locomotive owned by British Railways. I almost succeeded, except that the two 0-4-2T engines that used to shunt the docks in Aberdeen were scrapped just before my friend Ron Puntis and I got there in 1960. Also, I had what might have amounted to a phobia about telegraph or lighting poles sticking out of engine chimneys, which could result from poor selection of the photographer's position. So serious was I about this that, when I was confronted with a former LMS Beyer-Garratt articulated locomotive at Cricklewood depot which had a telegraph pole standing in front of the leading unit, I did not take its photograph. I never saw another of these enormous locomotives on BR and thus have taken no picture of one! Another lesson learned.

During the decade of the 1950s, steam reigned supreme over much of British Railways, except on the Southern suburban lines where green electric trains were the order of the day, and on a few isolated lines in the north. Living in Bournemouth and working at Eastleigh I had countless opportunities to record the Southern Region's steam locomotives on all their duties, main line, branch line, passenger and goods trains, in stations, depots and yards, in the countryside and in townscapes and docklands.

But I was also interested in the new and in the less-known. When diesel locomotives began to appear on the main line railways of Ireland, a few years before Great Britain had serious numbers of these, I was impressed by their acceleration, smell and apparent cleanliness. I loved the facility of sitting behind the driver in a diesel railcar and looking out through the windows in the front passenger saloon that enabled me to see the railway ahead almost as clearly as the driver could; modern diesel trains no longer give us that fun. I learned to photograph anything that was new, because very often the new locomotive or unit would soon be modified and its appearance changed to make it more practical or reliable, and the original would be gone for ever. For example, the BR Metro-Vick Co-Bos and the Scottish Region 'blue train' electric units were built with curved corner windows in their cab fronts, as were the later Trans-Pennine DMUs. These used to crack, and were difficult to replace, so BR replaced them with flat windows or removed them altogether. In the UK, white headcode discs and oil lamps on diesels gave way to panels with letters and numbers, then later on to bright electric headlamps, and much more recently to a triangle of lights. A red-glowing oil lamp attached to the back of each train, even on diesel and electric trains, was eventually supplanted by electric lamps embodied in the locomotive or carriage, and flashing electric tail lamps on locomotive-hauled trains.

But in the 1950s, headcode discs or lamps still told the signalman what type of train it was or, on the Southern, where it was going. British Railways embarked on programmes to improve some of its steam locomotives, with better exhaust systems, double chimneys to reduce back-pressure in the cylinders, and higher superheating of the steam to get more power from it, such that the engines' performances sparkled in the hands of good crews. My favourite locomotives, Mr. Bulleid's pacifics on the Southern Region, were rebuilt at Eastleigh to a more conventional form, and in my view, became even better locomotives. On the Southern, the fast London Waterloo to Bournemouth Central trains had their timings cut by ten minutes to cover the hundred and eight miles in two hours, and these were not lightweight trains, loading up to thirteen coaches.

Biased as I was – probably still am! – towards the Southern and its locomotives, I admit to being particularly fond of the 'Bournemouth Belle', an opulent train of Pullman cars that ran daily from London to Bournemouth and back, filled with the wealthy on business or on holiday. The Pullman cars in their umber-and-cream colours with gold lining looked superb, the attendants in their crisp white jackets added to the spectacle, and the air-smoothed 'Merchant Navy' class locomotives that pulled the train were equally fine in my young eyes. I have more pictures of that train than any other.

I was the first member of any known generation of our family to travel abroad. My first chance to do this was a trip with my colleague Mark Abbott to Ireland in July 1956. We spent a happy week in unusually good weather (most days) travelling around the main lines and

visiting engine sheds and three of the smaller railways. I was hooked, and went to Ireland again the following year for a more in-depth two-weeks tour when it rained every day, and have visited that lovely island lots of times since.

But it was my membership of the Eastleigh & District Engineering Society that took me to continental Europe by train and ferry for the first time. In October 1956, we went to the Renault car factory near Paris and the immaculate Brown Boveri factory in Baden, Switzerland. That trip included a train journey from Interlaken up the Jungfrau reaching the summit in a blizzard. The following year, the same group went to visit railway installations in Belgium, in Brussels and Liège, and my interest in foreign railways began to blossom.

A tour of Austria in 1958 with the Railway Correspondence & Travel Society (RCTS) introduced me also to the railways of the German and Austrian federal republics and to the wonderful scenery in the Austrian Alps. I realised when I got home and saw my black-and-white photographs that without colour I was not recording the Alpine scenery as the human eye saw it. I needed to embrace colour photography, which by then, thankfully, was becoming affordable in the form of 35mm colour slides. However, my Super Ikonta used 120-sized roll film, not 35mm, so I needed to buy an additional camera for colour work.

Thus I paid just £29 for a brand new Voigtländer Vito IIa folding 35mm camera with Zeiss f/3.5 Color-Skopar lens and Compur Rapid shutter. Because colour slides do not have the exposure tolerance of negative films, I also purchased a Weston Master III exposure meter so that I could more accurately measure the light in front of the camera before taking photographs. Much to my delight, my first film was evenly exposed throughout, and most of its images are reproducible today after nearly sixty years. My choice of slide film was Agfa CT18 because the images I had seen taken by other photographers rendered black locomotives black and not with slight colour casts of green, cyan or magenta as some other films tended to do. Modern authorities decry the keeping properties of this Agfa film, but having stored my slides over the years indoors at room temperature I have been pleased how so few have faded, particularly those from my earliest films.

In 1959, my friend Ken Shingleton and I ventured on a mammoth two-week tour that took in Holland, Germany, Austria, Switzerland, Italy and France. I was very satisfied indeed with the images produced by the Vito IIa camera, so much so that I went on using it for colour slides for twenty-eight years, not replacing it until 1987. I also used it occasionally over the years as a standby for my black-and-white camera.

By the late 1950s, my darkroom skills were improving and I was able to judge the exposure times under the enlarger reasonably well. I was developing my own black-and-white films, too. I had learned how to use my hands to shade certain areas of a print under the enlarger so as to bring out the sky tones, for example, or to hold back shadow tones to reveal some of the otherwise hidden detail there. My only real criticism of these methods, now that I am blessed with the reliability of digital print techniques in the twenty-first century, is that it was not easy in the darkroom to get absolute consistency of image quality when doing repeat prints from a negative.

Looking back over the 1950s, particularly in the later years of that decade, I can see that I produced some of my best black-and-white photographs in that period. In particular, the results I got from the Super-Ikonta camera were excellent, especially when I had acquired the Weston exposure meter. I had experimented with films of 100ASA (FP3), 200ASA (HP3) and 400ASA (HPS and HP5) and had eventually settled on Ilford FP3 film. FP3 was a fine grain film giving superb tonal separation and gradation, and in my view, was unsurpassed by anything put on the market since.

I often used my photographs to give slide shows to railway enthusiast groups, my membership of the Bournemouth Railway Club giving me the opportunity to learn and practise public speaking. I remember lending prints to my friend Nigel Hiscock for a talk he gave at our school. The pictures were projected from an episcope, sometimes mistakenly called an epidiascope. This was a device that lit up a print placed on its table and which projected the image onto a screen. The room needed to be well-darkened for the image to be clearly visible. Once I had taken some colour slides, I bought a 35mm slide projector and a screen. I was then able to show slides to audiences, basing the shows either on my travels or on specific railway subjects. This is something I still do, though in the digital age it is so much easier – using digital media there is no risk of dropping slides on the floor, of or putting them through the projector upside down or the wrong way round, something that bugs people watching slide shows even today!

Brownie box camera, 3¼in x 2¼in
As the 1950s began I was carrying my Brownie box camera around on my bicycle to places where I might see some interesting things on the railway. Salisbury was accessible by bike from Bournemouth in those days, road traffic on the A338 being less manic than today. At Salisbury in summer 1950 I took this view of 'Merchant Navy' class 4-6-2 35020 *Bibby Line* at the head of the 'Atlantic Coast Express'. It was taking water there before heading west with its heavy train over the fast but hilly West of England Main Line on to Exeter and Plymouth, on the way splitting into its many portions to serve multiple destinations. The low level from which the photograph was taken illustrates my short height at the age of twelve, compounded by the need to look down into the tiny viewfinder to see what I was photographing! This picture illustrates how good the lens of a simple and cheap box camera could be.

This was my first attempt at a time exposure. On the Brownie box camera, there was a time exposure setting in which the shutter could be held open at will. Inside Branksome sub-shed on a Sunday afternoon in February 1952, ex-LMS Class 5 4-6-0 44826, the engine for the next morning's 'Pines Express' from Bournemouth West to Manchester London Road, was resting at the back of the shed in partial shadow. I sat my camera on the front footplate of a Class 2P 4-4-0 that was standing on the next track, and held the shutter open for about three seconds. I like the result.

Before the Second World War, the Southern Railway ran special trains with Pullman cars for royalty and their guests travelling from Windsor to Ascot for the races. Only medium-sized engines could be used on those lines; the 1899-built Class T9 4-4-0 119 was specially painted green and polished for those duties. After the war, the engine was again painted green, this time in malachite, and it kept this colour when renumbered by British Railways as 30119. In its last years, it worked from Dorchester shed on local trains to Weymouth and Bournemouth, as seen at Bournemouth Central on 29 June 1952 just a few months before it was withdrawn for scrap.

Nagel Librette folding camera, 3¼" x 2¼"
The Southern Railway and Region built three prototype main line diesel locomotives, the first of which
emerged from the works at Ashford just over two years after the LMS 'twins' 10000 and 10001. The first
SR locomotive, 10201, was exhibited at the 1951 Festival of Britain exhibition on London's south bank. It then
joined 10202 working out of London Waterloo on trains to Bournemouth, Weymouth and Exeter. 10203
started work early in 1954. On 17 May 1953, 10201 brings an express from Bournemouth West to London
Waterloo into Bournemouth Central. In early British Railways days, between 1949 and 1956, corridor carriages
were painted a bright carmine red-and-cream livery and looked very jolly. By 1953 I was using my father's
Nagel Librette camera on permanent loan. Taking successful pictures of moving trains was now possible.

Britain's very first main line diesel electric locomotive, built at Derby in 1947, 10000 and its sister locomotive
10001 both spent a couple of years on the Southern Region from 1953 to 1955 working alongside the three
Southern 1Co-Co1s. 10000 was a regular on the down 'Royal Wessex' express for some time. The 'Royal
Wessex' started from London at 4:35pm with thirteen coaches. Six were detached at Bournemouth Central,
including the restaurant and buffet cars, and completed their journey at Bournemouth West. Two more
coaches were dropped off at Wareham in Dorset and were taken by a tank engine to Swanage, and the front
five coaches went on to Weymouth behind the main line locomotive. The photograph shows 10000 with the
train having left Bournemouth Central on its way to Weymouth on 2 July 1954.

Britain's only 'elevated railway' was that which ran south to north from Dingle to Seaforth passing nearly all of Liverpool's docks on the way. The Liverpool Overhead Railway opened in 1893 and was one of the earliest railways to use electric traction from the start, as well as being a pioneer in having electric light signals. In the 1950s, work had started in rebuilding the trains with more modern bodies at the railway's works at Seaforth Sands. One of the modernised units is seen approaching Pier Head station on 13 August 1954. The Royal Liver Building can be glimpsed in the background. The railway closed at the end of 1956 because the overhead structures needed heavy repair that could not be financed at that time.

My first photograph to be published was this one of the aftermath of a collision between two 4-6-0s at Bournemouth Central on the evening of 22 January 1955. The H15 was arriving with a stopping train from Weymouth. It collided with N15 30783 *Sir Gillemere* that had been started erroneously when its driver reacted to a main signal for an adjacent track instead of the shunting signal for his track. The following morning, Class H15 30485 was still lying at an angle. In this view, the errant N15 had been shunted out of the way and stands, minus smoke deflectors and its right hand cylinder, at the right edge of this picture. Bournemouth depot's breakdown crane was attempting to lift the front of 30485, but at twenty tons capacity, it was inadequate for that work and the team had to wait until Salisbury's thirty-five tons crane had arrived to join the Eastleigh one (on the left) for the final lift.

On a peaceful 9 April 1955, Urie N15 4-6-0 30742 *Camelot* approaches its stop at Christchurch just east of Bournemouth with a local service. Like many SR stopping trains in that period, the carriages were mainly of pre-grouping origin, in this case London & South Western Railway, apart from the SR Maunsell corridor coach at the back. The sharply curved track on the left was once part of a branch line from Ringwood, where it connected with the original Southampton to Dorchester route that avoided the Bournemouth area. It was only in the 1880s that the now well-known seaside resort grew large enough to justify a main line connection, the last link, the direct line from Brockenhurst, being completed in 1888. The Christchurch to Ringwood line closed in 1935.

Boscombe was to become the only station on the main line between London Waterloo and Bournemouth Central to close during the Dr Beeching era. Bournemouth West at the end of its short branch was also to close. In happier days, on 11 April 1955, I photographed a most unusual visitor to Boscombe in the form of Fairburn 2-6-4T 42096 calling with the afternoon stopping train from Bournemouth to Andover Junction via Eastleigh. The engines of this type that were allocated to the Southern Region normally worked only on the Central and Eastern Sections of the that Region. To carry the Southern's special headcodes, these engines were modified with two additional lamp brackets on the smokebox front; the Ivatt 2-6-2Ts on the SR and all its BR standard engines were similarly adorned.

In this busy scene at Eastleigh station on 6 July 1955, Urie S15 4-6-0 30500 rumbles through with a partially-fitted freight bound for Southampton Docks. These solid, strong engines regularly worked the sixty-wagon freights from the docks to the London area, either to Feltham or Nine Elms. On the right is a T9 4-4-0 on a short train for Portsmouth. Centre left an M7 0-4-4T stands at the rear of a push-pull train from Southampton Terminus to Alton, and on the extreme left a train of former Great Western stock arrives on a service for the Didcot line. I chose not to remove the slightly irritating lampposts from above the S15 because the engine's image is strong enough for these not to be problem.

Trains big and small pass at Eastleigh on a sunny evening on 4 July 1955. On the left, just pulling out of the station with a semi-fast train from Waterloo to Bournemouth, is Bulleid 'Merchant Navy' 35027 *Port Line*. Behind the engine is one of the eleven six-coach restaurant sets that were built for the Bournemouth main line in 1946-1947, identifiable by the side sheets extended downwards to below step board level. On the right, Ivatt Class 2 2-6-2T 41304 arrives with a three-coach Bulleid corridor set on a stopping train from Southampton Terminus to Alton.

At the north end of Shrewsbury station on 15 July 1955, ex-London & North Western Railway 0-8-0 49146 is about to move its freight train forward following a signal stop. The arrays of semaphore signals have long been a feature of this area and have survived well into the twenty-first century, as also have the former Great Western Railway signalboxes such as the one in the background. Replacement by modern signalling is now only a matter of time.

Looking very forlorn under a makeshift roof opposite Towyn Pendre depot on 16 July 1955 sits the original 0-4-2T of the 2ft 3in gauge Talyllyn Railway in North Wales. The locomotive was built by Fletcher Jennings in 1864 and was ninety-one years old in this photograph. No. 1 *Talyllyn* rested in this shed for many years, worn out but repairable. It has since been fully restored and is a regular and popular locomotive, serving well past its one hundred and fiftieth birthday.

On the recently-preserved Talyllyn Railway on 16 July 1955, Kerr, Stuart 0-4-2T No. 4 *Edward Thomas* takes water at Towyn Pendre before heading for the Wharf station to take on a limited-stop train for Abergynolwyn. The locomotive had spent most of its life on the Corris Railway near Machynlleth; when that railway closed, its two useable engines were acquired by the Talyllyn which enabled that railway to soldier on. The Talyllyn Railway survived on slate traffic and minimal passenger carryings until 1953. That year it was taken over by a preservation society, the first railway of many in the UK that became the heritage railways we love so much today.

Trains leaving the east Lancashire station of Colne, a former cotton weaving town, have to cross the valley of the Colne Water on this splendid stone viaduct when heading towards Nelson, Burnley and Accrington and points south and west. Back in 1955, the town still supported many cotton mills as seen in the background of this view of ex-Lancashire & Yorkshire Railway 2-4-2T 50652 heading west with the push-pull shuttle to Rose Grove on 21 July. Some of the small halts on this line had no platforms, just sleepers alongside the track from which passengers had to climb into the carriage using folding steps let down by the guard; the coach next to the engine had these beneath the inset double doors. Notice that at this time, the street lamps were still traditional gas lamps. Indeed, some of Colne's older houses still had a 110V DC electricity supply.

During a visit to the Liverpool Overhead Railway to gather information for my first published article, I alighted for a time at Herculaneum Dock station near the south end of the railway. The picture, taken on 18 July 1955, is full of railway interest. One of the original three-car trains accelerates away from the station and approaches a bridge over the British Railways tracks into Brunswick yard and depot, and then the tunnel that took the overhead railway to its underground southern terminus at Dingle. Prominent on the left of the photograph are two new carriages for export, probably to Africa. Under the LOR structure and against the boundary wall are two really old carriage bodies in use as offices or for storage, their short length suggesting they were once four- or six-wheeled vehicles.

The extensive docks at Southampton were rail-connected by tracks running through the streets. Along Canute Road on 29 October 1955, Stroudley Class E1 0-6-0T 32689 trundles a freight heading from the Eastern Docks to the Western Docks. Interestingly, the engine carries a 75A shed plate on its smokebox door, indicating its allocation was to Brighton depot, but by this date it was actually allocated to Southampton Docks shed. The sharply-curved tracks in the foreground led to Southampton Town Quay.

Zeiss Super-Ikonta 532/16 folding camera, 2¼in square
Rebuilding of the Bulleid 'Merchant Navy' class engines began at Eastleigh Works with the first, 35018 *British India Line*, being outshopped in February 1956. The locomotive became Nine Elms depot's favourite for the shed's star duty, the 'Bournemouth Belle'. With twelve heavy Pullman cars in tow on 2 April that year, the competent machine climbs the 1 in 99 of the incline between Christchurch and Pokesdown on the approach to Bournemouth. The Southern's express locomotives were well-managed by their depots and crews and rarely made unpleasant quantities of dark smoke, exhausts usually being clear as in this picture. It may seem geographically unlikely, but all trains had to approach the seaside resort of Bournemouth from either direction, east or west, by running uphill!

Two Bulleid light pacifics stand at the Up end of Bournemouth Central on 21 April 1956. On the left is 'West Country' class 4-6-2 34105 *Swanage* on an express to London Waterloo. 'Battle of Britain' class 4-6-2 34064 *Fighter Command* waits in the bay platform to take over a later working. I sometimes ask railway enthusiasts to explain the difference between the two classes. Thankfully, most nod wisely and say that there is no difference – they are just two different series of names among a class of one hundred and ten locomotives. This low angle of view shows detail of the bull-head rails and chairs of that period as well as the mechanisms of two SR-type shunting signals.

A low angle serves to give the impression of a main line locomotive in this view of 4-6-2 No. 10 *Doctor Syn* of the Romney Hythe & Dymchurch Railway in Kent. This fourteen miles long, fifteen inch gauge railway uses one third size steam locomotives and delights its passengers with views across the English Channel, the Dungeness flats and the Romney Marsh. This locomotive has since been rebuilt with a taller chimney and cab, but in 1956 it retained its original proportions that followed the lines of a Canadian 4-6-2. The chassis and working parts of the two Canadian-outline locomotives of the RH&DR were actually the same as those of its British-outline engines.

On the second day of my first visit to Ireland in early July 1956, Great Northern Railway (Ireland) Class PP 4-4-0 42, of a class introduced in 1896, arrives during a heavy downpour at Strabane in Northern Ireland with a stopping train for Londonderry Foyle Road. The unusual turntable in the right foreground has two track gauges, the main line 5ft 3in at the lower level and 3ft gauge in the centre. This was an innovative device for sliding a specially designed container (wagon body style) from a narrow gauge Country Donegal Railways flat wagon on to a similar broad gauge wagon, a very early attempt at intermodal working. Note the plethora of wires hanging around the scene. Some photographers would have me remove them using Photoshop. Perfectly possible, but did not they help to date the scene to the pre-modern age?

One of the GNR Board's finest express engines, blue-painted three-cylinder Class VS 4-4-0 208 *Lagan*, begins to move a heavy train bound for Belfast out of Dublin Amiens Street station. There were five of these engines, built in 1948 by Beyer Peacock in Manchester. They were a three-cylinder simple development of the five compound locomotives delivered by the same company in 1932. The steam jets at rail level indicate that the driver has the steam sanders working to place a layer of sand on the rails in front of the large driving wheels to enable the engine to grip the rails and avoid wheel slip. Across the front of the smokebox door is a hinged nameplate that, when swung upwards and locked in position, announces the 'Enterprise' service, non-stop between the two capital cities. One of the GNR's diesel railcar sets is at the adjacent platform.

Never let it be said that diesels always have cleaner exhausts than steam locomotives! This is Córas Iompair Éireann's Co-Co diesel A25 starting away from Cork Glanmire Road station in July 1956 with a Sunday morning special for hurling supporters. The engines in these sixty locomotives that were ordered in one batch from Metropolitan-Vickers of Manchester were Crossley eight-cylinder two-stroke machines with what the company described as 'exhaust pulse pressure charging'. This used the pressure of one cylinder's exhaust output to raise the air input pressure in an adjacent cylinder. The engines vibrated badly, causing damage internally, and whole fleet was re-engined with General Motors engines in the late 1960s.

On 16 September 1956, a special train ran to and from Weymouth for the Ian Allan Group. On the way back to London, the train is seen climbing the 1 in 60 of Parkstone bank between Poole and Bournemouth. The train engine is one of the wide-cab 'West Country' 4-6-2s, which is being piloted over this quite difficult route by ex-London & South Western Railway Class T9 4-4-0 30727, clearly enjoying itself because its safety valves are blowing off despite the effort being put into the climb. I have no record of the pacific's number; it may just be that I am no longer a natural train-spotter!

This train is out to sea! Ryde Pier Head station stands behind this train that is pulling along the pier to reach land at Ryde Esplanade before continuing south to Ventnor, in 1956. The locomotive is Class O2 0-4-4T W36 *Carisbrooke*. On the left is the pier's tramway shuttle, the trams' petrol engines being replaced by diesel engines a year after this picture was taken. In the right background is the paddle steamer *Ryde* backing off the pier in readiness to strike out on the crossing to Portsmouth Harbour and the railway connections to London and Bristol. Today the tramway is derelict and the main railway runs as a conductor rail electric line using 1938-type former London Underground trains in two-car formations.

This is the first photograph I took on the continent of Europe. It shows the inside of the train shed at Le Havre Ville station just after we travellers had walked there from the ferry terminal early in this October morning in 1956. The train that has just arrived has eight ancient four-wheeled coaches – the first I had ever seen – and the locomotive is British-built (North British Locomotive Co.) 2-8-0 140C 186. The train in the left background is the 08:40 express to Paris St. Lazare. Two of the four-wheeled coaches were derailed when the stock of the local train was shunted out of the station – my first sight of a continental derailment!

This view struck me as I emerged from the subway at Baden station after our visit to the Brown Boveri factory there. Framed by the platform awning, ancient Class Ae3/6 electric locomotive 10662 was waiting to depart with our train for Zürich. The light was poor as the rain fell relentlessly but my Super-Ikonta camera recorded it well on Ilford HP3 film with enough shadow detail. The locomotive is nicely framed, and the station sign leaves no doubt as to the location.

ABOVE: Faced with the western corner of the triangular junction at Branksome station, the driver of West Country 4-6-2 34106 *Lydford* has clear signals for the route that will take the train to Bournemouth Central rather than the other line (left) that drops down to Bournemouth West. The train is a morning service from Weymouth. The fireman has let his side door swing out from the locomotive so that it is out of gauge!

LEFT: During a holiday with my grandparents in Lancashire I ventured to the depot at Bolton – with a permit – and was invited to climb up the coaling tower to get a better view! The main shed here had thirteen tracks, indicating how busy the railways were even in those days. The locomotives on view are, from left to right: a Stanier 2-6-4T, used on local passenger services between Manchester Victoria and the Lancashire towns; a LMS 4F 0-6-0 goods engine; a former War Department 2-8-0 freight locomotive, 733 of which were acquired by British Railways after the war; another 2-6-4T; a Stanier Class 5 4-6-0 for the heavier expresses in the area; a former Lancashire & Yorkshire Railway goods 0-6-0; and another 4F. The 3F 'Jinty' 0-6-0T at the bottom of the picture shunts the coal and ash wagons as required.

In early July 1957, nicely humped over one of Cork's two lifting bridges across branches of the River Lee, is former Great Southern & Western Railway 0-6-0T 217. The 0-6-0T is bringing a stock transfer train through the city streets en route from the yard at the main Glanmire Road station to the station at Albert Quay that served the western part of County Cork. This street tramway was the only rail connection between the two systems, all part of Ireland's 5ft 3in gauge main railway network. The west Cork system was closed in the 1960s, and today the bridge carries road traffic only, though the main Albert Quay station building remains intact. The locomotive was one of a class designed under the direction of H.A. Ivatt, who later moved to the Great Northern Railway in England.

LEFT: Ignorant as I was about foreign railways at the time, being just nineteen years old in 1957, I thought this was a typical Belgian steam locomotive as it approached on a long freight train and stopped for signals in Liège Guillemains station. It is actually typically Prussian, being a Class G.8 war reparation locomotive given to Belgium by Germany after the First World War. It did look nice however, having been painted in SNCB's light green livery. The locomotive is facing Belgium's steepest main line incline up to the small station of Ans; no doubt a banking locomotive would attach itself to push the train from the back, probably another Prussian type, either a 0-10-0T or 2-8-2T.

BELOW: My friend Gerald Stone and I visited the Isle of Man in summer 1958. Gerald was keen for me to try colour photography and gave me one of the Ferrania colour slide films he was carrying, a 120-sized film that would fit my Super-Ikonta. I duly tried one film, which was processed when I got home with reasonable results. Thankfully, although the slide today has chemically changed and now has a deep magenta colour cast all over it, the wonders of computers and Photoshop have enabled me to produce this adequate image of a pleasant scene, the 2-4-0T *Polar Bear* running on the Groudle Glen Miniature Railway near Laxey. At this point in my photographic progress, I was not ready to convert from black-and-white to colour.

Amid the excitement of my first visit to Germany and Austria, this time with the Railway Correspondence & Travel Society in September 1958, our carriages from the 'Loreley Express' were shunted out of the main station at Cologne (Köln) and on to the Hohenzollernbrücke, the famous bridge over the River Rhein, so that they could be moved to a different platform. While on the bridge, more than one of us tried to photograph this ex-Prussian P.8 4-6-0, Deutsche Bundesbahn (DB) 38.3066, leaving on a local train on the adjacent track. At that time, repairs to the bridge, which had been badly damaged by the Allies during the war, were well advanced but only two tracks across it were operational. The other two were brought into use before the following summer. I like this picture even though one British enthusiast leaning out of the window is in the way. I guess he helps to lead the eye to the P.8. The magnificent Gothic cathedral looms hazily in the background.

This is quite the most extraordinary train I have ever photographed! We were just about to leave the city after visiting the depot of the Graz Köflacher Eisenbahn (GKB) at Graz in southern Austria when this apparition of a freight train arrived from the south. The leading locomotive, 0-6-0 674, was built in 1860 and so was ninety-eight years old when seen in 1958. It had been built for the Austrian Südbahn just thirty-one years after Stephenson's *Rocket*, yet it had a working life of over a hundred years. It now rests in the Hungarian Transport Museum in Budapest, and it's not the only survivor of its type. Wonderful! The second locomotive was a youngster by comparison, having been built in 1904 and was just fifty-four years old. It was a two-cylinder compound 2-8-0, 56.3242. For some decades, the GKB had acquired and operated locomotives that were surplus on their railways of origin, and was thus a haven for enthusiasts of historical steam locomotives in the 1950s and 1960s.

A nice British anachronism that survived into the early 1960s was the Hayling Island branch a few miles east of Portsmouth. The bridge that carried the railway onto the island was this long and somewhat rickety-looking single-track structure near Langstone harbour; BR always omitted the final 'e' on the nearby Langston Halt. The bridge imposed a severe weight restriction on trains crossing it, such that the only locomotives that BR could muster in the south of England that were suitable were the Stroudley Class A1X 'Terrier' 0-6-0Ts. One of these sprightly performers is pictured, 32646, that was covering some of the branch trains in 1958, with 32677 taking over at Havant for each second trip on the more intensive weekend service. The middle carriage, S1000S, is an experimental BR suburban second produced in Eastleigh Works with a body made up of fibreglass-resin sections, probably the only item of modernity on the branch line!

The earliest batch of BR standard Class 7 'Britannia' 4-6-2s was allocated new to Stratford for Norwich line express trains, and revolutionised speeds and timings, bringing the Liverpool Street-Norwich time within two hours for the first time. On Sunday 1 November 1958, 70008 *Black Prince* was receiving due attention from a gang of young cleaners outside one of Stratford's sheds. A feature of the standard classes was the high running plate, well clear of the coupled wheels to give easy access for oiling and maintenance. On engines with smaller coupled wheels such as the 9Fs and Class 4s, a lower running plate height might have looked aesthetically better, as it did on the rebuilt Bulleid pacifics. Stratford depot had an allocation of over 400 locomotives at that time, being Britain's biggest depot with several sheds and workshops spread over a large site in east London.

Great Western railwaymen and enthusiasts together would tell you that there was no express engine in the UK better than a 'King' class 4-6-0 – we were always a bit partisan about our favourite classes. As a Southern man, I saw the 'Kings' as outwardly impressive and competent performers, but with some engineering drawbacks that other railways' locomotives avoided. This is 6002 *King William IV* arriving at Westbury on 9 October 1959, with a Sunday express train from London Paddington to the west country.

Zeiss Super-Ikonta 532/16 folding camera, 2¼in square: black-and-white
Voigtländer Vito IIa folding camera: colour
I surprised myself with the success of my first film of 35mm colour slides, of which this is one. I tried out my new camera together with the essential Weston Master III exposure meter, and immediately obtained consistent results. This is ex-Southern Railway 'Lord Nelson' class 4-6-0 30863 *Lord Rodney*, one of the two that were not modified with extended smokeboxes, standing outside Eastleigh shed on 28 April 1959, waiting for its next duty. The two oil headlamps are placed ready for it to take over an inter-regional train. Normally, SR locomotives ran with white disc headcodes in daylight hours. The Agfa CT18 colour slide film gave quite accurate colours, this being a good rendering of British Railways dark green.

This image was more of an experiment. I was photographing trains coming and going at Paris Gare du Nord on 3 September 1959. In the case of these push-pull suburban trains, the sun was almost in my face, but I wanted to record one in any case, and this is the result. Dramatic? It shows up one of the limitations of colour slide film in that there is virtually no detail in the deep shadows. The engine is de Caso 2-8-2T 141TC 60.

It was the trip to Austria in 1958 that had convinced me to take up colour photography so as better to record the superb scenery in the Alps. On 25 August 1959, my friend Ken Shingleton and I spent a day on trains climbing from Interlaken in the Swiss Bernese Oberland up to the Jungfraujoch, Europe's highest railway station at 3,466 metres above sea level. The third railway involved in that climb is the Jungfraubahn, a metre gauge rack line. One of the JB's new electric units arrives at the interchange station of Kleine Scheidegg overshadowed by the bulk of the Eiger mountain, the north face deep in shadow. The Abt toothed rack between the rails enables pinions on the train to engage and propel the train up the very steep gradients. They also engage with the train's brake pinions, adding some certainty to its ability to stop.

Another limitation of colour slide film is the lack of brightness when pictures are taken in poor light. At around 6:30am on 12 September 1959, I was waiting time before joining a factory tour in Manchester and chose to spend it picturing the old L&YR electric trains that used to run between Victoria and Bury Bolton Street. Leaving Woodlands and heading towards Bury, this unit of five wide carriages dating from the early twentieth century emerges from the mist. These trains collected electric current at 1,200V DC from a third rail using side contact, unique in the UK. At 10ft 2in width, these carriages were the widest in the United Kingdom. This route is now part of the Metrolink tram network.

CHAPTER 3

THE 1960S – DIESEL'S RISE AND STEAM'S DECLINE

The reign of steam locomotives on the railways of Great Britain and Ireland, and in many western European countries, ended in the 1960s. This event gave a boost to railway photographers everywhere to record steam locomotives at work before that spectacle could no longer be seen, or so most people believed.

Others welcomed the advent of new forms of traction and accepted that diesel and electric trains, which did not raise photogenic clouds of exhaust – at least, not when working properly – posed a different challenge to photographers. How could we create photographs that included these very different trains that would be both interesting and even pictorial? I accepted that challenge and tried by means of varying picture compositions to set diesels and electrics in scenes of which they would be an integral part. The absence of any visual indication that a train is moving makes a non-steam train photograph dull if there is nothing to put the train in context. No longer is the train on its own sufficient to make an exciting picture. My photographs of the Irish A25 at Cork and the ex-L&YR EMU in the last chapter perhaps make the point clearer.

Dr Richard Beeching became chairman of the British Railways Board and led the search for more railway efficiency in the early 1960s, with often controversial results. The impact of closures of uneconomic railways led to more photographs being taken on threatened routes such as the picturesque Somerset &

Dorset line. New trains emerged including the liner trains that carried the modern ISO containers that BR had not embraced until then, the genesis of the modern Freightliner. The 'merry-go-round' coal trains were a huge efficiency step-up when compared with the traditional coal trains of loose-coupled, unbraked wagons that were, truly, decades out-of-date even by the early 1960s. The most visual impact of the Beeching era was British Railways' adoption of its shortened name, British Rail, and a more modern livery for its locomotives and passenger trains, the newly-developed shade of rail blue being the dominant colour that was to hold sway for the next quarter of a century. All these changes were subjects for railway photographers to record.

The 1960s were the years in which, following the end of my engineering apprenticeship, I became a young railway technician, an Associate (later a Corporate) Member of the Institution of Mechanical Engineers and then developed towards becoming a manager in the field of traction and rolling stock maintenance. My career took me to Brighton in 1960, Derby in 1963, where I met Mary, a former Swindon girl who became my lovely wife in 1965, thence to Eastleigh again from 1965 to 1969 and lastly to Cardiff.

In 1962, having got very good results from my 35mm Voigtländer colour camera, I decided it was time to embrace 35mm black-and-white photography as well. My choice of a new camera was not a wise one, it transpired. The UK-made Corfield Periflex 3 had a good lens and a fast, focal plane shutter. It had two faults, which Corfield in Northern Ireland seemed unable to put right each time I sent the camera for correction. There was a difference in focus distance from one side of a negative to the other when the lens was at or near full aperture at f/2 and, even worse, the two halves of the shutter sometimes caught each other up when I was using a fast shutter speed, resulting either in one side of a print being darker than the other, or even half the negative being blank. That was a pity, because the focal plane shutter was designed for a maximum speed of 1/1000th second, just right for photographing any trains at high speed. I was cautious about excess grain in the resulting prints off 35mm negatives, so I started by using Ilford's Pan F film. This was very fine grain, which it achieved by having a slow speed, rated at 50ASA. As the Periflex had a lens with a wide maximum aperture of f/2, I judged this would adequately compensate for the slower film speed.

Because of its faults, and because we needed the money, I sold this camera in 1965 to help us buy our new dining room table. From then to 1970, that is until I could afford to buy another camera, my trusty Voigtländer IIa had to cover both my colour and black-and-white photography. This meant careful forward planning. I was using black-and-white for my definitive railway pictures and most locomotive portraits, and colour for family pictures, holiday scenes and occasional railway changes, such as the new BR train liveries of the day. The Voigtländer had a maximum aperture of f/3.5, so regular use of Pan F would not be practical. I went back to using Ilford FP3 and the results were better than I had expected.

I had been a member of the Bournemouth Railway Club since 1948, and by 1960 I was its fixtures secretary.

Apart from visits to locomotive sheds around the UK, in 1962, I ran the club's first trip to Scotland which also included the Isle of Man. In 1961, 1963 and 1968 I led its first and subsequent continental tours. In 1962, with my fellow member Alan Trickett, I enjoyed my first experience of the lovely country of Portugal and its enchanting railways, and a year later took my colour camera to Ireland for the first time.

I also made a determined effort to photograph the developments at Eastleigh works in the later 1960s when the carriage works was combined into the smaller locomotive works site. The combined works became for a while Britain's most efficient location for carriage overhauls. I am glad I did all that because the pictures came in handy about forty years later when Peter Stanton and I co-authored a book recording the history of Eastleigh Locomotive Works.

An interesting test of photographic technique came about in 1962. The Bournemouth Railway Club ran a box camera competition, using a Brownie-style camera loaned by a senior member. The idea was that each member taking part would have the camera for one week and would pass through it just one 120-size black-and-white film, giving eight chances of getting a result. My turn came in February, when I was working at Brighton. My only spare time that week was in the dark evenings, not exactly what one chooses for such a limiting camera! One evening, I went down to Brighton station and walked to the outer end of the island platform that curves towards the line to Portsmouth. There I tried to photograph the colour light signals that glimmered hopefully. Having taken about six photographs of these I was ready to go back to my lodgings when, as I walked back towards the concourse, I noticed a three-coach Horsham train standing against the adjacent platform. At each end was an Ivatt Class 2 2-6-2T, one detached near the buffer stops, and one ready to take the train on its next trip. Steam from the lead locomotive was drifting up into the station roof, silhouetted by the brighter lighting around the concourse. It made a good picture. I placed the box camera on a repositioned luggage trolley, composed the picture in the viewfinder, lifted the lever that set the camera to 'time' and gave it a six seconds exposure. This turned out to be the only good negative of the set!

I was surprised how sharp the resultant print was at whole plate size, so I sent it with a caption to the magazine *Trains Illustrated*. The picture duly appeared in print, much to my surprise. To this day, the editor has never been told that he published a picture in a quality magazine from a mere box camera! It did not win the Club's competition, however, coming in second.

Mary and I moved from the Eastleigh area to Cardiff in 1969. To the modernised but still shrinking British Railways, I added the photographic opportunities of the myriad of National Coal Board mines and railways in the South Wales valleys. And we were not far from the collection of 'scrap' steam locomotives that rested in Dai Woodham's yard at Barry Island. Visiting coal mines in those days was not the difficult exercise that it would later become. Discipline was fairly lax at several of these locations, and ad hoc visitors almost encouraged. The presence of several working steam locomotives was a big attraction. I toured most of the South Wales areas with my cameras over the next two years – okay, that takes me into Chapter 4! – and then I wrote an article for a magazine which I entitled *Steam in my valley*. The reactions I got from local Welsh colleagues and enthusiasts were unexpected. One said, 'It's not *his* valley!' Another, at a Stephenson Locomotive Society meeting in Cardiff, complained:

'Don't write about these engines – we don't want *everybody* coming to look at them!'

One problem in the 1960s, a problem that only revealed itself decades later, was that the colour film I was using, Agfa CT18, faded over time. It happens that my late-1950s colour slides are still as vibrant as ever, but the films I used in the middle to late 1960s include many slides in which the colours have faded, the greens in particular. The colour balance within the greens has changed such that attempting to boost the saturation in Adobe Photoshop has no effect; the former grass greens remain pale turquoise. Strangely the rendering of BR's rail blue seems as strong as ever. I also found that in later films the contrast was if anything greater, and the slides sometimes displayed sky tones bleached out.

Another change that was immediately noticeable was the 'upgrade' from Ilford's superb FP3 black-and-white fine grain film to the new FP4. Living in South Wales, the light in some of the valleys – Mary and I tried to visit every one! – was often not great. Using the very fine grain Pan F film at 50ASA that had accompanied me in my former Periflex camera was out of the question. FP4 produced more contrasty images than FP3, and some of the latter film's subtle tone variation had been lost, I felt. Do not misunderstand me – I got some very good results with FP4, but it just did not have the tonal sensitivity of its illustrious predecessor.

I had been able to buy a second-hand Rollei 35 camera in Cardiff for my black-and-white work and this served me very well for fifteen years. Its 40mm Zeiss lens was slightly wider-angle than the 50mm lenses I had become used to, but that was no real problem. The camera was so compact when its lens was retracted that it fitted in a jacket or trouser pocket, as did the Voigtländer.

All these years, I was developing and printing my own black-and-white films, setting up the darkroom in a bedroom or in the loft. I had found Microdol X developer to be good, and later switched to Promicrol which was a little less contrasty. The Eastleigh & District Photographic Society had also taught me the adage, when related to developing negative film; 'Just enough exposure AND NO MORE; just enough development AND NO MORE.' I tried that scheme and it did work. Negatives were finer-grained. Looking back at the negatives of that period, I do sometimes see a lack of shadow detail, so it was not always the right thing to do. As it happened, the gutsy images that emerged with FP4 film somehow compensated for that.

All through the years with photography, we had to adjust each time a manufacturer changed the formula of a film or chemical. Sometimes our image quality suffered while we got used to another change. Looking back, I wonder whether all the changes were necessary. It is a bit like today's challenges of keeping up with changes in information technology, computers and software!

After my third Irish trip, I felt that I had enough material to write and illustrate a book. I approached Ian Allan Publishing who accepted the idea of a book entitled *Irish Railway Album*. It had to be black-and-white as colour would have been too expensive. I subsequently persuaded the publisher that a colour picture on the jacket would help sell the book better, and that was done. My first book therefore appeared in 1968 with a nice portrait of former GNR(I) 4-4-0 No. 171 in blue livery sitting on the turntable at Portadown on the cover. Looking back with the wisdom of age, I can see several errors in the book that came from the naïvety of youth. I did not realise at the time, for example, that the title's initial letters, as printed boldly on the front cover, spelled out *IRA*, an organisation to which I have no affiliation. The book is still however a good record of what I had seen in those heady years of the decline of Irish steam. It includes pictures of active steam, diesel, electric and horse traction, and trains on three different track gauges, none of which was the Stephenson standard of 4ft 8½in!

Black-and-white: Zeiss Super Ikonta 532/16 camera (to October 1962)
Black-and-white: Corfield Periflex 35mm camera (from October 1962 to 1965)
Colour: Voigtländer Vito IIa 35mm camera (plus black-and-white after 1965)

For two weekends in March and April 1960 the Southern Region's Bournemouth main line was blocked for engineering work at New Milton. All trains were diverted between Brockenhurst and Bournemouth via the 'Old Road', namely the original main line through Ringwood and Wimborne – now closed – and thence via Poole. This meant that trains from London had to approach Bournemouth from the west instead of from the east. Normally 'Schools' class 4-4-0s were not permitted to run over this route due to their 21ton axle load, but an exception was made on 3 April for this stopping train from Eastleigh headed by 30910 *Merchant Taylors*, seen crossing the causeway opposite Poole Park and just beginning the 1 in 60 climb up Parkstone bank on the approach to Bournemouth. Poole gasworks and the new power station dominate the background; both have long since gone. This causeway has since changed vastly. Much land has been reclaimed to the left of this picture. There are now streets of houses where the sea was lapping up against the railway embankment. The place on which I was standing is also not publicly accessible, being inside private property.

In early April 1960, I set about recording the Eastern Region scene in a number of areas, as that Region was relatively unfamiliar to me. Just after I alighted at Hatfield station, the main line signals cleared for this Down express, heading north behind A4 4-6-2 60020 *Guillemot* with a string of clean maroon BR mark 1 coaches in tow. I always wished that British Railways had placed the 'smokebox door' numberplates on this very special locomotive class just above the middle bottom lamp bracket. Placed so high up as it is on the streamlined front, it breaks up the smooth lines of the locomotive. It must also have caused some unnecessary air turbulence at speed.

Between the tunnels at Hadley Wood, WD 2-8-0 90024 clunks along with a southbound loaded train of ballast hopper wagons. This was in April 1960, not long after the main line had been widened from two to four tracks through this pinch-point on the East Coast Main Line. The north tunnels are visible in the background; interestingly, the new tunnel is on the left (west side) and the old one on the right, whereas the new tracks are on the right, the old ones appearing to have been realigned to reach the new tunnel.

The track through Hadley Wood and its three tunnels had only recently been duplicated to four tracks when I visited the area in 1960. An Up express is pictured between the two northernmost sets of tunnels. It is headed by new English Electric Type 4 D209. Five of these heavy diesels were allocated to the East Coast Main Line at this time.

Most photographs of the Beattie 2-4-0 well tanks show them on their specific regular duty, working the Wenford Bridge branch from its clay quarries, for which they were the only locomotive authorised to work that line due to its civil engineering constraints. I was surprised on 23 July 1960 to see 30586 being used to shunt passenger rolling stock at Wadebridge station, releasing the two-coach B-set from its ex-GWR 2-6-2T train engine. All three of the surviving Beattie tanks had received general overhauls at Eastleigh Works in the late 1950s. They had started their lives in the nineteenth century on suburban workings out of London Waterloo. The whole class, with the exception of these three locomotives, had been withdrawn from service well before the First World War. On the right is a water column, used for topping up the water tanks in steam locomotives. The brazier alongside it is fired up in winter to prevent the water in the column from freezing.

The main locomotive works across the UK were originally built to be largely self-sufficient. At Eastleigh Works near Southampton, for example, the iron foundry was still making iron castings for steam locomotives in 1960. This picture shows molten iron being poured into the largest casting type that the works produced, a pair of cylinders (the inside and one outside) in one casting for a three-cylinder Z class 0-8-0T. This casting needed two two-ton ladles of molten iron, and it was critical that the second one was ready quickly to ensure that the iron in the mould was still hot enough to blend with that being poured from the ladle. Looking at how the men are protected, modern health and safety experts would have a fit!

The half-roundhouse engine shed at Inverness displayed what must be the grandest entrance feature of any British depot. The entrance portico carries the depot's water supply in a large tank across its roof. This 1960 view shows a new BRCW/Sulzer Type 2 Bo-Bo backing into the depot, ready to couple to the even newer BR/Sulzer Type 2 standing in the background. In later years, this depot was abandoned in favour of using the buildings of the former Highland Railway Loch Gorm works as a diesel locomotive maintenance and repair depot.

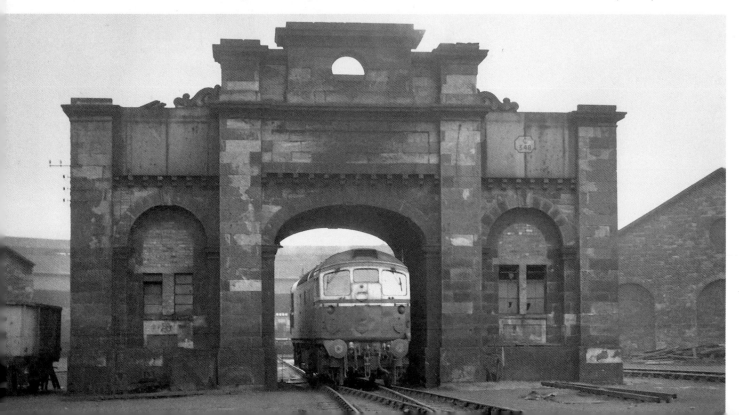

In 1968, the Peak Main Line in Derbyshire was closed between Matlock and Millers Dale, by the direction of Barbara Castle who was then the Labour Government's transport minister. This cut the main line that linked the East Midlands cities of Nottingham, Leicester and Derby with the metropolis of Manchester. All trains were either abandoned or re-routed, stone trains mainly using the Hope Valley Line. In fact, Dr Beeching had only nominated the route as 'not for development'; he had however identified the need to remove all stopping passenger trains from it. The reality was that the line closed north of Matlock, and south of that county town only stopping trains remained, quite the reverse of what the Beeching reports had proposed! In 1960, before all this happened, a northbound coal train of loaded 25ton hopper wagons plods uphill through Millers Dale behind Stanier 8F 2-8-0 48225; the exhaust from its banking engine is visible at the rear of the train, the ruling gradient on this route being 1 in 90.

In autumn 1960, I ventured to Grantham and the east coast lines through Boston and north to Grimsby, an area with which I was quite unfamiliar. The morning fog was beginning to lift when I arrived at Grantham. Gresley Class O2 2-8-0 63955 soon came storming uphill with a southbound mineral train as the sun began to penetrate. The two covered vans behind the engine form a 'fitted head', providing a little additional braking power for this otherwise unbraked consist. The infrastructure at Grantham that this picture reveals is interesting. Signals were colour light, with 'feathers' mounted at 45 degrees where diverging routes had to be indicated. Electric lamps were raised on the original gas lamp poles, as seen on the Up platform to the right. Even a relatively medium-sized station and junction like Grantham had several signalboxes, the one in view being labelled 'Grantham North'. The main line tracks are heavy, flat-bottom rails but with wooden sleepers. Happily, the signal and the platform lamp frame the train in the composition, and there is just enough exhaust and escaping steam to show movement.

At the south end of Grantham station, A3 Pacific 60047 *Donovan* is ready to restart an Up express train as A4 60022 *Mallard* approaches at speed with the 'Flying Scotsman' bound for Newcastle and Edinburgh. An L1 2-6-4T blows off in the yard. The station lampman goes about his task oblivious of the steam activity. There is a lot of sky in this composition, possibly too much, but I wanted to include all the rising steam in the middle of the picture as well as that impressive telegraph pole standing in the top left corner.

Once the mist had cleared at Grantham it was a nice day. A3 4-6-2 60111 *Enterprise*, in very clean condition, rolls through the station towards the depot. For reasons which I do not fully understand, Grantham was one of the places where locomotives were scheduled to be changed, even though in hindsight they ought to have been perfectly capable of running from start through to destination!

By the time I reached Lincoln, the weather was becoming cloudy. I was delighted to get this shot of B1 4-6-0 61160 crossing a narrow inlet to the canal basin, with the lovely cathedral looming in the near distance. I particularly like all the wharf and warehouse type buildings that speak to us of former times. This image shows how the colours of Agfa CT18 film made in the 1960s has faded. Despite my efforts to increase colour saturation using Photoshop, the grass on the left has a turquoise hue. Many others of my slides from that era are far worse in this colour distortion.

An unusual practice that still took place on BR's Scottish Region in the early 1960s, a carry-over from LMS days, was the swapping of the restaurant car from the morning Inverness to Kyle of Lochalsh train to the opposite working about half way through the journey. In summer 1960, I witnessed this operation at the remote station of Achnasheen. The Stanier Class 5 4-6-0 working the train from Kyle was detached on arrival at Achnasheen, ran forward, and backed onto the restaurant car which was at the back of the train from Inverness to Kyle sitting on the adjacent track. In this picture, the locomotive has just taken the restaurant car forward and is backing it onto the Inverness-bound train on which I was travelling. How bare the area would look without that row of antiquated telegraph poles!

In the shed yard at Kittybrewster, north Aberdeen, stand Class J36 0-6-0 65277, formerly of the North British Railway, and a B1 4-6-0. The J36 is standing over one of the two parallel ash pits. This enabled the ash from the fire to be raked out from the ashpan under the firebox and dropped into the pit between the rails or alongside the track. A labourer would later come along with a shovel and wheelbarrow and empty the ash from the pit, loading it into the seven-plank wagon on the right of the picture.

The ascent of Shap incline from the south, where the West Coast Main Line crosses part of the Pennines, was one of the London Midland Region's legendary climbs. 'Jubilee' 4-6-0 45627 *Sierra Leone* is fully stretched in taking its eleven-coach train up the final 1 in 75 near Scout Green and its three-cylinder exhaust beat reaches a crescendo as the train approaches the camera. A strong side wind blows the exhaust to one side, while the hazy weather almost hides the distant fells. The train is probably one from Birmingham to Glasgow.

On 5 August 1961, I wanted to photograph a 'Deltic' on the Up 'Flying Scotsman', and went with my lineside pass to Finsbury Park. I was delighted when the train hove into view past Grantham 5 signalbox headed by none other than the doyen of the class, D9000. The locomotive carried the headcode 1A35, meaning it was a Class 1, an express passenger train, heading for destination A (London) and 35 was the unique train number for the southbound 'Flying Scotsman'. Dedicated 'Deltic' enthusiasts will notice that in this picture D9000 has no nameplates, and that the BR emblem is mid-way on the bodyside. When the locomotives were named, the nameplates replaced the crests, and smaller crests appeared on the cabsides beneath the locomotive numbers. In the right background are stabled rakes of Gresley quad-art suburban stock. These were normally worked by former GNR N2 class 0-6-2Ts; I regret never having photographed one of these in action.

In the opposite direction on the same day, passing Finsbury Park No. 6 signalbox, is Gresley A3 60067 *Ladas* working the Down 'Yorkshire Pullman'. BR had modified the locomotive with double-Kylchap exhaust system and smoke deflectors. Apart from the end coaches, the Pullman cars on this train were new ones from Metro-Cammell developed from the BR mark 1 carriage design. Riding on Commonwealth cast steel bogies, one of these coaches later gave me my first experience of 100mph running with diesel traction, and it rode very well at that speed. The order for these new vehicles had not included guard and luggage space, so older Pullman cars graced both ends of this train and also the 'Tees-Tyne' and 'Queen of Scots' Pullman trains.

I arranged and led the Bournemouth Railway Club's first overseas trip in 1961 which included train travel in Holland, Germany, Luxembourg, Belgium and France. While in Germany, the tour included a ride on the unusual Wuppertal Schwebebahn, the monorail in which the commuter cars are suspended from the overhead structure that spans the Wupper river for much of the journey along the winding valley. This view of an approaching train was against the sun which was shielded from the camera by the overhead decking. This 'railway' has replaced its hanging cars twice since this picture was taken. The railway once or twice has suffered from occasional closures following collisions by heavy road vehicles with the diagonal struts that support the tracks.

The year 1961 saw the end of steam haulage of the 'Golden Arrow', the Pullman train that linked London Victoria with Dover for the ferry to Calais, from where passengers boarded the similarly-named 'Flêche d'Or' for Paris Nord. My boss in Brighton, John Click, was on the footplate of rebuilt 'West Country' 4-6-2 34100 *Appledore* as it headed the southbound train through Beckenham Junction. The Bulleid pacifics introduced electric lighting on Southern steam locomotives, fed by a steam turbo-generator under the cab. On this luxury train, accommodation for the guard was in the rearmost four-wheeled parcels van! One of the tracks on the left of this picture is now part of the Croydon Tramlink system.

February 1962 was not the best time of year to take good pictures with a box camera, but the rules of the competition in which I took part insisted on giving each participant one week to put one film through the camera donated for the occasion, and this was my turn. I was pleasantly surprised at this result! An evening train bound for Shoreham and Horsham was headed by Ivatt Class 2 2-6-2T 41261 with its smoke and steam being blown up into Brighton station's overall roof. A time exposure of about six seconds sufficed to produce this picture, of sufficient quality for it subsequently to be published as a serious work in the magazine *Trains Illustrated*!

On the cold afternoon of 17 March 1962, former London & South Western Railway S15 4-6-0 30502 struggles manfully with an up freight that it had drawn out of Eastleigh's Allbrook yard and was beginning the sixteen-miles-long 1 in 252 climb on the main line to London, its effort not being helped by a leaking cylinder drain cock. The ruling load for these tough old engines on the Southampton to London main line was sixty wagons. Some wag had chalked the words 'Flying Scotsman' on the smokebox door!

After travelling on the Portuguese broad gauge local train from Porto to Leixões in summer 1962 my friend Alan Trickett and I were walking southwards along the shore when we unexpectedly came across this metre gauge terminus at Matosinhos as we approached the harbour. The branch train engine was one of the two oldest articulated Mallet 0-4-4-0Ts on Portuguese Railways (CP), No. E152, and the four-wheeled coaches were the only ones we saw on the narrow gauge on that visit. In this almost timeless scene, the engine had run round its train, and was ready to depart for Senhora da Hora on the metre gauge main line when these schoolchildren rushed up to join the train. This branch line was soon to be an early closure, but now modern standard-gauge trams link Porto with Matosinhos, albeit by a different route and terminating short of this spot. They provide a frequency of service undreamed of in the 1960s.

Travelling by train and boat all the way from Portugal back to Bournemouth, I had reached Paris and had joined the boat train to Le Havre at St. Lazare station. I watched the evening suburban trains come and go, though I was too naïve to understand that the artist Monet had, in his time, been fascinated by the sunlight shining into the station's trainshed. Nonetheless, this scene caught my eye as I leaned out of the carriage window, and I was lucky to record a three-cylinder Class 141TB 2-8-2T of the former Ouest railway propelling its train at the start of its journey to the city outskirts. Unusually, another of the same class was facing the opposite way with another train, helping to lead the eye to the departing train which is nicely framed by the end of the station structure. This is one of my all-time favourite photographs.

The second phase of the Kent Coast electrification which was launched in late 1962 caused many Southern Region steam locomotive classes to be withdrawn and rendered extinct, including the grand 'Lord Nelson' class 4-6-0s designed under the direction of Richard Maunsell. On 11 August 1962, one of the last two survivors, 30862 Lord Collingwood, drifts into Winchester with a Saturday Up express from Weymouth and Bournemouth to London Waterloo. Fortunately, 850 Lord Nelson is preserved, and has proved to be an excellent performer, particularly when handled by crews from Carnforth and Carlisle Upperby.

In October 1962, having purchased a Periflex 3 35mm camera with f/2 lens, I tried it out in low light conditions to record the 'Brighton Belle' electric multiple unit Pullman train as it approached Brighton from London Victoria. Photographed with the lens opened right up at f/2, I was amazed at the apparently long depth of focus, enabling almost the whole length of the train to be rendered reasonably sharply. However, had the train been pictured from the opposite side, crossing the field of view downwards from right to left, the result would have been much less sharp overall because the camera had an in-built faulty alignment between the lens and the film plane. This picture is the only one I have seen that shows all three of the five-car Pullman sets; the spare 5BEL unit can be seen in the background alongside the carriage sheds.

Saturday 8 September 1962 was the last summer Saturday on which long distance holiday trains between the North of England, the Midlands and Bournemouth were routed via the Somerset & Dorset line. That included the 'Pines Express' which was the only long-distance train to run on weekdays all the year round over the S&D. From the following Monday, it was rerouted to run via Basingstoke and Oxford, gaining its former route north of Birmingham. I photographed the very last 'Pines Express' to traverse the steeply-graded S&D line as it passed the village station at Midford in the Mendip hills. In response to a special request from members of the Bournemouth Railway Club, British Railways provided Class 9F 2-10-0 92220 *Evening Star* to work the train between Bath and Bournemouth. This competent locomotive gave a splendid performance on this last run, including very spirited climbs of the gradients on the line. At that time, this was the only daily train between Bournemouth and Manchester. In 2017, the towns are linked via Oxford and Birmingham by an hourly service!

Wanting to photograph some locomotives from the East German railways (Deutsche Reichsbahn) I headed for Bebra in West Germany in October 1962 and got there just in time to witness this arrival from Leipzig. Having just crossed the border from the east, DR 4-6-2 01.218 arrived with a through train for Cologne formed of five modern West German (Deutsche Bundesbahn) coaches. This handsome two-cylinder pacific was basically unmodified from the original Prussian design of 1925, with deep smoke deflectors. The overall black livery was offset by clean red wheels, valve gear and frames; indeed, even the air reservoir in front of the cab was bright red. These colours are standard for all German steam locomotives that belong(ed) to either DR or DB, or even the Austrian Railways. No. 01.218 was changed at Bebra station for a DB locomotive for the rest of the journey into West Germany. The uniformed personnel on the platform by the train included passport and customs control staff, ready to process the international travellers.

Also at Bebra, later the same morning, the opposite working from Cologne to Leipzig arrived behind three-cylinder 4-6-2 01.1102, one of the top link express engines of DB. In this train, the carriages were DR vehicles. This engine was replaced by DR 01.218 for the run to Leipzig, deep inside the Deutsche Demokratische Republik (DDR). What looked like a very large diameter chimney on the 01[10] in fact concealed an annular ring containing the blower exhaust. The typical German signalbox and semaphore signals were quite foreign to British eyes.

I took part in the Bournemouth Railway Club's 1963 tour to Paris and Brittany, with the aim of experiencing the metre gauge Réseau Breton railway. This railway connected several towns around the Breton peninsular with the interior, five lines converging on the town of Carhaix where the depot and works of the line were to be found. Carhaix had been the starting point for this mixed train to Rosporden, worked by 4-6-0T E330 which detached itself from the train at several stations to shunt wagons in or out of the consist, which it was doing when pictured at the small station of Gourin. When this small engine arrived at Rosporden, it was soon afterwards utterly dwarfed by a huge standard gauge Class 241P 4-8-2 that came in alongside with a train from Paris to Quimper.

Also in 1963, a visit to Ireland gave me the opportunity to take photographs of some of the last steam trains there, mostly in Northern Ireland because by the summer of that year there were no regular scheduled steam workings in the republic. At Portadown on 25 June, this large Class SG3 0-6-0 of the former Great Northern Railway (Ireland) was starting off southbound with a very short goods train. This is the only one of my photographs that has ever appeared on a postage stamp, being used on the 78p stamp as part of the Classic Locomotives of Northern Ireland series issued by Royal Mail in summer 2013.

On the same day, fifty-years-old 4-4-0 171, formerly named *Slieve Gullion* was being turned on Portadown turntable. Although carrying the branding CIE on the front buffer beam, this engine was one of a small group that had just been sold to the Ulster Transport Authority (UTA) to alleviate a pending steam locomotive shortage in the North. When finally withdrawn from service, 171 was taken into the ownership of the Railway Preservation Society of Ireland (RPSI), and has seen several periods of main line action in recent years, being an excellent and favourite main line performer on the Society's special trains.

The former main line that linked Derby with Manchester and carried through trains from London St Pancras and from Nottingham crossed this iconic viaduct over the beautiful Monsal Dale in the Derbyshire Peak District. Dull weather did not deter me when this 9F 2-10-0 emerged from Headstone tunnel onto the viaduct in summer 1963 with a mixed freight train. The seven Presflo cement wagons at the head of the train are a reminder of Derbyshire's limestone quarrying and processing industry; this industry still prospers today even though the line closed in 1968 between Matlock and Millers Dale. The viaduct now carries the Monsal Trail cycle and walking track, a very popular recreation facility. Even the tunnels have been reopened for cyclists and walkers who can experience them with interior lighting up to 8pm each evening.

Another Midlands activity that kept 9F 2-10-0s gainfully employed was the job of transporting iron ore from the Northamptonshire ore quarries to the steelworks at Scunthorpe. 92133 gets a grip with a loaded ore train through Wellingborough station on the Midland Main Line in summer 1963. When the Appleby Frodingham steelworks were modernised in the 1970s, the use of higher-grade imported iron ore shipped into the country through Immingham Docks replaced this traffic and iron ore extraction in the UK ceased. In modern times, Wellingborough station's five platforms have been reduced to three, and the carriage sidings now form the car park. The background is unsharp because of a problem with the Periflex camera that is described in the text.

Dieselisation spread across the UK in the late 1950s and early to mid-1960s. Among the heaviest diesel locomotives were the aptly nicknamed 'Peak' 1Co-Co1s which weighed 133tons. In this view at Grindleford on the Hope Valley Line, D84 *Royal Corps of Transport* calls with a Manchester to Sheffield stopping train of three BR mark1 coaches which in total weigh over thirty-five tons less than the locomotive!

One of the heaviest trains on the Bournemouth main line was the 'Bournemouth Belle'. In this view, taken just after the Down train had passed Lymington Junction west of Brockenhurst, rebuilt 'Merchant Navy' class 4-6-2 35017 *Belgian Marine* has eleven Pullman cars in tow plus two bogie vans, a total tare weight of over 500tons. Nonetheless this competent locomotive was expected to cover the one hundred and eight miles from London Waterloo to Bournemouth Central, with a stop at Southampton Central, in just two hours. 35017 was coupled to the Region's self-weighing tender at this time, a means of measuring coal consumption.

Not only was the 'Pines Express' rerouted from September 1962, but it had also been dieselised by 1966 when this picture was taken at Southampton. Brush Type 4 D1711 in its original two-tone green livery leaves Central station with the Manchester Piccadilly to Bournemouth Central service made up of mark1 coaches in the former maroon and the new rail blue-and-grey colours, the latter style having been introduced as part of Dr Beeching's efforts to modernise BR. Prominent in the right background is Southampton power station. This used a couple of tiny electric locomotives to move wagons around its yard, and there was a rail connection across the road to just short of Southampton Tunnel. The power station and its railways have all long since gone. An arterial road now runs where I was standing.

Towards the end of steam in the London area of the London Midland Region (LMR), 9F 2-10-0 92086 emerges from under the coaling plant at Cricklewood depot, while an Ivatt Class 2 2-6-2T awaits attention. The LMR built several coaling plants like this at its major depots around the country. This one appears to have dragged skips up the side to tip their contents into the hoppers, whereas some other plants lifted complete wagons. These plants were less labour intensive than other methods, their one disadvantage being that, as the coal fell into the hoppers and then into tenders and bunkers, it broke into smaller pieces than suited many steam locomotives. The photo was taken with the Vito IIa camera following disposal of the unreliable Periflex camera.

The Bournemouth electrification scheme got off to a rocky start caused by the late delivery of some of the express electric multiple units. Locomotive haulage was scheduled for a few Waterloo-Bournemouth-Weymouth trains, such as this Down express passing through Eastleigh behind electro-diesel Bo-Bo E6104 in autumn 1968. Ten of these locomotives were produced by rebuilding E5000 series electric locomotives with a Paxman diesel engine generator set, enabling a locomotive to work away from the conductor rail areas when needed, for example in docks and goods yards. The return run would have the locomotive at the back, propelling push-pull style. It's interesting to compare this empty-looking station with the busy appearance it has in today's much more crowded railway!

To celebrate the 25th anniversary of the founding of the Bournemouth Railway Club in 1968, I led a continental tour that took in the Netherlands, Germany, Luxembourg and France, seeking out places where steam locomotives were still in use; this was a year after steam had finished on BR's Southern Region. As the BRC party left Lille on an electric locomotive hauled train for Paris, our train overtook this North-American-built 141R 2-8-2 roaring away on a local service. Those were the days when main line carriages still had drop windows that one could lean out from – not recommended for safety reasons! – which enabled quite a lot of railway photography to be achieved that would be impossible today with our modern, sealed, air-conditioned trains.

CHAPTER 4

THE 1970S – FASTER TRAINS, INDUSTRIAL STEAM, AND TOURIST RAILWAYS

The 1970s brought new horizons – and considerable family disruption – with successive career moves to South Wales, Yorkshire and later to Scotland. This pressure was compounded by the birth of our youngest daughter, Claire, just after we had moved to Doncaster. It was also not helped by the huge hike in mortgage rates to 13% soon after we had moved to Glasgow four years later, and we had already stretched ourselves financially to move there.

The decade had begun with us exploring the South Wales Valleys, an area we had never previously visited and one that contained a myriad of fascinating railways, many of them not being run by British Rail. I soon became familiar with commuting from our local station at Radyr into Cardiff on a train of two three-car diesel multiple units from Merthyr. My work took me to traction depots around the whole of the Western Region, a railway that was still relying on diesel hydraulic locomotives for some of its traffic movement, though diesel electrics were already established in significant numbers. South Wales freights, for example, were very much in the hands of Class 37 Co-Cos, often in pairs, shifting coal up and down the valleys between mines, washeries, smokeless fuel

plants – very smoky, these! – the coastal docks and steelworks, often in sets of thirty-plus modern 'merry-go-round' air-braked hopper wagons. I often wondered at the economics of moving coal from a mine in one valley to a washery in another and then perhaps to a processing plant in a third, all the time descending to Radyr yard to run round and reverse direction! We often had the unusual prospect of watching loaded coal trains go up and down the same valley. Anyway, it kept the railways running in the area.

Our weekends were spent taking our car up almost every valley, where we quickly discovered that many coal mines owned sidings and railways worked by steam locomotives. The variety of pictorial backgrounds from old industry to rural sheeplands and bare mountains was a haven in which to photograph these newly-discovered workings. The variety of steam locomotive types that the National Coal Board ran was considerable. For example, at Mountain Ash in the Cynon valley, the six steam locomotives there were all of different types. Further west, in complete contrast, the Maesteg NCB district was more rational as all its hard-working steam locomotives were of the one type, the common austerity 0-6-0ST.

Photographing industrial railways has its own techniques. I am particularly drawn by large complicated industrial backgrounds that sometimes tower above the local landscape; steelworks and coal mine pithead gears come to mind in this context. They can be shown to dwarf the trains that serve them. Also, the atmosphere surrounding some plants could be heavy and dark with smoke or fug. There are some pictures in this chapter that show that. For steam locomotives in these surroundings, the low speeds at which they shunt or transfer trains of wagons lend themselves to plenty of exhaust rising into the sky, so there are, or were, many pictorial possibilities in industrial areas. Nowadays there are few if any places like this in the UK, with the possible exception of major steelworks and power stations. Access to these to get close enough to photograph railway action is likely to be difficult. That is why some photographers have travelled to places like China in recent decades, where industrial steam locomotives can still be found if you know where to look. By the time this book is published, there is not likely to be very much left anywhere in the world.

In summer 1970, Mary and I braved the long journey by train and ferry to Austria, taking our two small children and Mary's father, Jack, with us, our son Tim still needing a push-chair. While the railways and scenery in Austria were highly photogenic, I still only had one camera, so I alternated between colour and monochrome films as best I could. On the way home, when we stayed for a night in Ulm in southern Germany, I was able to take some photographs of DB steam locomotives working passenger and freight trains. By that year, 1970, most of these engines were looking somewhat unkempt, not as I remembered German steam from the later 1950s when we were transfixed by clean black locomotives with the moving parts and wheels in bright red, something I did not see again until the East German authorities relaxed their objection to railway photography there in the late 1970s.

The overall experience of these long journeys with very young children was stressful and put us off doing overseas journeys until they were older. We did not venture abroad again as a family until 1978. By then, we judged that our three children were mature enough to understand something of what they were seeing, and it was good to watch Julia, our eldest, buy an ice cream in Calais with the whole transaction successfully completed in her schoolgirl French.

Late in 1970, I at last had enough cash to buy a second-hand Rollei 35 camera to replace the Periflex that I had sold in 1965. I used this compact 35mm camera for black-and-white photography and my trusty Voigtländer resumed its life of full-time colour slide work. This was the era when the Ilford company replaced its FP3 film with FP4. Thankfully, the slower speeds of trains in the Welsh valleys enabled me to continue to use this relatively slow film in all weathers at 100ASA. I set up my darkroom in the loft, and filled boxes with prints of the railways of the NCB and of BR Western Region.

Looking back, as I scan in some of the photographs from this decade, I realise that the 1970s represented my nadir of negative quality. Using FP4 film developed in either Microdol or Promicrol led to some negatives that today exhibit significant grain, particularly in plain areas such as skies. They also possess a tendency to scratch easily when being pulled or pushed in and out of the long envelopes in the negative carriers of the day; this has necessitated my spending time with Photoshop removing scratches from some of the images that I have scanned for this chapter and the next one.

We only lived two years in South Wales, and left with fond memories of which the photographs from that time are a good reminder. We then had four-and-a-half years based in Doncaster. My cameras roamed with me around the Doncaster Division of BR and on the East Coast Main Line. I was able to record the variety of diesel locomotives and railcars that BR employed there, and found particular fascination in getting to grips with photographing the freight scene which I had previously rather neglected. On occasions, with my friend Alan Thorpe whose company we much enjoyed, I visited mines in the Yorkshire coalfield where steam locomotives were declining quite sharply. After 1976, when we had moved again, this time to Scotland, Alan visited us quite often from his home in Bournemouth, and we continued to look for the remaining steam-shunted coal mines in the central belt. The last steam on NCB in Scotland survived in use at Bedlay colliery into the 1980s. Bedlay was just twenty-five minutes' drive from our home in south Glasgow.

My attempts to get good photographs of electric trains, both locomotive-hauled and multiple unit, weren't entirely great, though I did at least try! I became familiar with the quirks of the so-called 'blue trains', the three-car EMUs that radiated out of Glasgow. My regular commute was over the short distance from Cathcart to Glasgow Central. At least the two big terminus stations in Glasgow were photogenic, and I spent quite a lot of leisure time trying pictorial angles under their cavernous roofs. I also did a lot of 'news' photography, enabling railway magazines to keep their readers up to date with short pieces about the changes on the railways in Scotland. I missed the demise of that magnificent station, Glasgow St Enoch, and the wonderful potential it would have offered me for some pictorial railway photography. The station had a wide and impressive overall roof, partially glazed, that was demolished to make way for a retail development. The latter eventually was built at great cost and had … an overall glazed roof! Do we never learn?

The 1970s witnessed the rise of some significant heritage railways around the UK. Scotland had relatively few of these, though we did get to visit the Bo'ness & Kinneil line near Edinburgh. I recall being there with our family one afternoon when the railway's fine, blue Swedish 4-6-0 was working. Mary had recently bought a new white coat and was wearing it when the 4-6-0 suddenly primed as it moved off. Black smuts everywhere. Talk about poor Mary being long-suffering! Another lesson learned. We also, later, reached the Strathspey Railway from Aviemore, though it always seemed to rain when we were there.

More positively, BR allowed the Scottish Railway Preservation Society (SRPS) to run some of its locomotives and its mixed bag of carriages over BR tracks, so there was sufficient main line steam activity to keep a railway photographer pleasantly occupied. I was particularly struck with the potential when one day the Society paired the North British Railway 0-6-0 *Maude* – named after the First World War general, you understand – with the sole surviving Gresley three-cylinder 4-4-0 *Morayshire*. Other operators also sent their steam locomotives to handle special trains around Scotland, so we glimpsed *Flying Scotsman* once, and quite frequently had the pleasure of seeing how well the Scotland-based A4 60009 *Union of South Africa* performed.

Steam also starred at the 1975 'Rail 150' event at Shildon. I had arranged a week-long trip for the Bournemouth Railway Club on which we called in at preserved railways en route between Bournemouth and Co Durham. Our journey on the Keighley & Worth Valley Railway was undertaken after sunset.

We enjoyed a spectacular display of sparks raining on the surroundings as our Stanier Class 5 forged uphill to Howarth, where we stayed in a pleasant, if cramped, hotel. For the main 'Rail 150' event, we had booked places in the field south of the lineside at Shildon and so viewed the cavalcade from the sunny side. This had been a cheaper option than the more upmarket reserved seating, which was on the north side looking straight into the sun. It did not take long for the photographers among us to elbow our way politely up to the lineside fence, and we got excellent views of all the exhibits steaming past, with the exception of the *Locomotion No. 1* replica which was partially obscured by a trolley on a nearer track that was carrying media people with their TV cameras.

In our Doncaster house, I had managed to find room and time to build a small 00-scale model railway, measuring eight feet by five feet, yet including a double track main line circuit, a branch to a terminus with goods yard and depot, and another branch leading down to a hidden area I called the docks. All these were vertically separated by means of inclines of 1 in 30. Photographing that model railway in 1975 was a challenge as neither of my cameras had any means of accurately measuring close focal distances, nor did I have a flash-gun. My colleague Phil Jones stepped in, bringing his single-lens-reflex (SLR) Praktica camera for the job. This was my first introduction to SLR work. We used bounced flash, aiming the flash-gun at the box room's sloping ceiling so as to get even light distribution. I did

try direct flash for a couple of model locomotive portraits, which certainly looked significantly brighter. With Phil's help I learned to make sure the camera was steady on a firm tripod, and to use a slow shutter speed to allow the light of the flashgun to reach the film through the lens before the shutter closed. I think we settled on an exposure of 1/60th second at f/22, the small aperture set so as to make sure the image of the models were sharp.

The results overall were reasonably good, indeed good enough fully to illustrate my article in the magazine *Railway Modeller*. Happily, this little model railway was dubbed the magazine's 'Railway of the month' and one of my pictures was on the cover. When we moved to Scotland in 1976, I cheekily wrote an article about how I had run all the model trains away from the terminus onto the main line one-by-one as part of a make-believe closure of the branch line. Surprisingly, the *Modeller* also published this, possibly tongue-in-cheek! It is nice to know there is a sense of humour in modelling circles.

About the time we moved to Scotland, I had given up on the tendency of Agfa CT18 film to give me slides with blank skies, and switched to Kodachrome 200 colour slide film. This had less contrast than the Agfa film and was sufficiently good for me to stick with it for at least five years. I didn't like the 'cheap' Kodak card mounts, but the resulting slides proved to be much more consistent in quality. They have retained their colours through the past forty years without noticeable degradation.

Colour: Voigtländer Vito IIa 35mm camera
Black-and-white: Rollei 35 camera with 40mm lens
Not long after we had moved house to South Wales, we explored the Taff valley north of our home in
Radyr and discovered a steam locomotive working in the nearest coal mine, Nant Garw. With the industrial
background adding to the smoke, one of the mine's three 'austerity' 0-6-0STs moves a rake of 16ton coal
wagons in the process of making up a train that will, later, be collected by a BR Class 37. The mine's output
was graded into fine and coarse coal; most of the fine seems to have ended up in heaps on the ground.

Our eldest daughter, Julia - aged fifty at the time this book is published! – stands transfixed at her first sight of a National Coal Board industrial steam locomotive at work among the eastern valleys that led south towards Newport. Barclay 0-6-0ST *Islwyn* was making up a train of open wagons at the Talywain depot. These wagons would, later that morning, be occupied by a group of enthusiasts for a trip up the side valley from Talywain to Blaenserchan colliery. By this date, 21 March 1970, steam on British Rail's standard gauge lines had been non-existent for nearly two years.

Former BR steam locomotives frequently found extended employment after being sold to concerns such as the NCB. Approaching Blaenserchan with a trainload of railway enthusiasts enjoying light rain in open wagons is 0-6-0 pannier tank 7754, having managed the steep climb from the valley bottom at Talywain with the Barclay banking. Several pannier tanks of this type were used by the NCB during the 1970s. This picture was something of an artistic experiment, using the siding-end buffer stops as a frame for the train. I must have stopped the Rollei 35's lens down considerably to get both the buffer stops and the train reasonably in focus. A good little camera, so it was!

Venturing further up the Cardiff valleys to the Cynon in January 1971, I first espied this little green Avonside 0-6-0ST through a gap in the roadside houses, and had to take a closer look! *Sir John* was shunting the yard at Mountain Ash and appeared almost like a ghost from a past century. The home-made chimney did nothing for its aesthetics, but added nicely to the engine's quaintness. NCB had been granted use of some former BR railway tracks in the valley in order to reach other mines at Aberaman and Penrhiwceiber, which the NCB had named 'Penrikyber' because of its ignorance of Welsh spellings and apparent unwillingness to ask the locals.

By 1972, ex-GWR 0-6-0PT 7754 had moved to Mountain Ash following contraction of the NCB railway at Talywain. While *Sir John* was pausing during its local shunting work, 7754 was being prepared to work up the main line to Aberaman, a duty it shared with 'austerity' 0-6-0ST No 8, and sometimes a diesel 0-6-0. The Peckett 0-6-0ST stabled out-of-use behind *Sir John* was *Sir Gomer*. There was also a larger Avonside called *Lord Camrose* which was always in the back of the shed during my visits to Mountain Ash. A Barclay 0-6-0ST arrived there fresh after overhaul in my last few months in South Wales, nicely painted light green but with its name shown as *Llantanam Abbey* missing out the '*r*', another example of NCB's inability to spell Welsh names correctly. No two of the six or more locomotives kept at Mountain Ash during my stay in South Wales were ever the same!

On its way back from working wagons to Aberaman in April 1971, 0-6-0ST No. 8 drifts past the smokeless fuel plant at Abercwmboi. This view shows the valley on a relatively clear day – it frequently became much worse atmospherically. Local folklore suggests that birds used to fly backwards to avoid being choked by the smoke hanging in the air.

In summer 1971, our young son, Timothy, makes an appropriate gesture of excitement when faced with yet another WD-style 'austerity' 0-6-0ST and a 0-4-0 diesel shunter in the small shed at Blaengarw, north of Swansea. Very often at South Wales collieries, steam locomotives were preferred to diesels when the latter were not always as reliable.

Aberaman sidings echo to the exhaust of former GWR 0-6-0PT 7754 as it enters the yard with a load of coal that it has brought up the valley from Mountain Ash in April 1971. Most wagons used by BR in this area were standard 16ton unfitted mineral wagons. In the siding on the right are two NCB internal-user wagons and also a longer-wheelbase 21ton BR wagon. A crane in the background is loading coal from the dumps into wagons for onward movement.

'Austerity' 0-6-0ST *Linda* makes a strong effort to propel a rake of loaded wagons towards the washery at Maesteg in September 1971. I was surprised at how hard these engines were driven on the admittedly steep gradients in this area. Sensibly, the local NCB had standardised on this WD type for the heavy loads and relatively high mileages that these engines endured. They carried small nameplates on their tank sides, each being a girl's name.

A study of the ash pit at Pontardulais NCB shed in September 1971 shows the residue after several weeks of raking out ash from the line's working 'austerity' tank and its small Barclay 0-4-0ST. The latter engine is in the background shunting wagons alongside the small single-road engine shed that was sufficient for the two locomotives in working order there. This railway ran several miles from the lower valley exchange sidings to the Graig Merthyr mine nestling up in the hills.

Near the top end of the Rhondda Fach, the smaller valley that branches off the Rhondda Fawr, lay Maerdy colliery, incorrectly spelled by the NCB as 'Mardy', which was shunted mostly by the unique, large Peckett 0-6-0ST. This chunky machine is seen in September 1971 lugging a loaded rake of wagons towards the upper end of the yard as a move towards making up another train for despatch via BR. Like many of the steam locomotives that survived in South Wales into the 1970s, this engine is preserved.

A day out from South Wales at a weekend in 1972 enabled the Boocock family to visit the Severn Valley Railway. This was running two trains that day, one headed by a former LMS 8F that had been repatriated by BR from war service in Egypt, and the other formed by GWR diesel railcar No. 22, seen here leaving Bridgnorth. In my view, this train was by far the more interesting subject for my camera by virtue of its rarity as an ancient working diesel railcar. It may be small in the picture, but the trees frame it nicely and its GWR livery helps it to stand out from a rather low-contrast background.

On moving to Doncaster, my working area was the Doncaster Division of BR's Eastern Region. My work required visits to the traction depots in the Division, including Lincoln. This photograph is on the route that included Lincoln St Marks station which has since closed, with trains rerouted into Lincoln Central. In 1974, English Electric Type 4 40051 was heading a London King's Cross to Grimsby and Cleethorpes service made up of mark 2 pressure-ventilated coaches. Because this route was used by frequent heavy freights including oil and steel trains from Immingham and Scunthorpe, the track had heavy rail on concrete sleepers, albeit in the 1970s the nearer main line track was not yet continuously welded. On the left is a coal depot in which a rake of 24ton coal hopper wagons is being unloaded over a below-track hopper feeding a system of augurs for loading lorries. For me, it is the details of the lineside equipment and the rake of hopper wagons in the siding that make the picture interesting. For others, it may be the Class 40.

Being called out in the middle of the night was one memorable part of my job while working and living at Doncaster and later in Scotland. Late one evening near Beverley, a taxi driver had got his vehicle stuck on an occupation crossing made up of railway sleepers. Fortunately for him, he was walking away when a northbound train from Hull to Scarborough ran into and destroyed his taxi, the leading vehicle of the train becoming derailed in the accident. The Doncaster breakdown train was summoned to help re-rail the Cravens DMU involved. At night and in foggy conditions, I was fortunate – or skilled? – enough to get a reasonable image from a hand-held shot at maximum lens aperture of f/3.5 and probably around 1/30th shutter speed or less. It is surprising how much light there actually is in an urban environment at night, particularly with fog around that can reflect the local street lights into the clouds.

One of the perks I had in mid-career was to attend the senior management course at Woking in 1972. This course included a visit to Hamburg and Berlin to witness German management methods. During time off one evening, there was an opportunity to visit Hamburg Hauptbahnhof to watch the train movements. The station was reasonably well lit, and it was possible to rest the Rollei 35 camera on a footbridge parapet to take a long, probably one second, exposure of this view across the station. In the foreground was the red Mitropa dining car on a train from West Berlin, the train being formed of dark green DR stock from East Germany. These trains, like the one the course members were to use to reach Berlin two days later, were so arranged that there were no passenger stops during passage of the DDR, these trains being known as *Korridorzüge*. Signal checks were always well away from station platforms. Engines on our train were changed from diesel to steam in Wittenberge freight yard. The trains in effect passed through a virtual corridor preventing the public from joining or alighting while traversing the communist state. During passage of the DDR, each carriage had a pair of armed guards on board who were alert for any attempts to join or leave the train.

It was not too far from home in Doncaster to visit the Keighley & Worth Valley Railway in West Yorkshire. This railway then was yet young, having first opened to the public in 1968. At that time, some of its locomotives bore liveries quite different from their former colours when working on BR or elsewhere. Notable in this respect was the USA 0-6-0T 72, the former Guildford shed shunter, which the K&WVR painted a bright fawn colour with a very American silver smokebox and chimney, a style which the author felt suited it very well. In this guise, 72 gained the nickname 'Tornado' due to its rousing roar when opened up to haul trains up the line's steep gradients. It is seen here leaving Keighley around 1972 amid typical West Riding hills and industry.

Among the NCB collieries I visited in Yorkshire was Wheldale, which kept its 'austerity' 0-6-0ST *Antwerp* in immaculate condition. This is one of the Hunslet tanks that the NCB modified with Kylpor exhaust and 'gas-producer' firebox systems, as exemplified by the inverse taper to the chimney. The locomotive shed is to the left of the photograph. Under the loading bay is a rake of internal user coal wagons. Also on site was a train of small side-tipper wagons that were used to remove spoil from the mine. Many coal mines produce considerable quantities of spoil as part of the exercise of gaining access to the actual coal seams. These spoil trains were usually sent to the edge of a mining site and tipped onto a slag heap, or what the Scottish mines called a 'bing'.

An excursion hauled by A4 4-6-2 *Bitterne* was run over BR metals to Malton where the participants joined buses that took them to Grosmont for trips on the recently-opened North Yorkshire Moors Railway. Two special trains were run on the NYMR, the first hauled by newly-restored ex-North Eastern Railway Class P3 0-6-0 2392. Producing a stirring exhaust column, the P3 approaches the hamlet of Esk Valley and takes a run at the foot of the 1 in 52 incline that replaced Stephenson's original and much steeper rope-worked incline; the course of the original incline is now part of a walking route up to Goathland.

Getting to grips with the 1 in 52 incline past Esk Valley while hauling the second train of enthusiasts that day is former NCB 0-6-2T 29, a design used among collieries in the north-east that was based on a successful Taff Vale Railway type. This is a strong little engine, well suited to the heavy work needed to take trains along this classic among British heritage railways.

In preparation for the official opening by Her Majesty the Queen of the modernised steelworks at Appleby-Frodingham, Scunthorpe, the empty Royal Train rounds Hexthorpe curve on the approach to Doncaster on its way from Wolverton via the West Coast and Midland Main Lines and Sheffield to north Lincolnshire where it would await the next day's event. When occupied by royalty, the Royal Train headcode would be 1X01, but as an empty train the leading locomotive, 25068, carried the reporting number 1X00. Note the leading locomotive's white-painted buffers and tyre rims. Next day the actual royal engine was a specially cleaned Immingham-based Class 47; its black buffers were adorned with a broad white rim round each, a style often used in Germany at that time, and which looks less messy than all-white buffers after being shunted against other vehicles. The platform on the left of this picture was part of the closed station at Hexthorpe.

The supply of iron ore to the modernised steelworks at Scunthorpe changed from the former use of indigenous iron ore from a local quarry and from Northamptonshire, and instead used higher-grade imported ore that came by ship via Immingham Docks, beginning in 1974. New train sets of twenty-one 100ton wagons, each train grossing 2,100tons in traffic, were built for this work, headed by pairs of Class 37s. The wagons, owned by British Steel, were loaded three at a time under large hoppers that dropped a measured seventy-three tons of ore into each wagon, the train being moved up in stages until all twenty-one wagons were loaded. The run to Scunthorpe included the 1 in 93 climb to the steelworks junction. This pair of 37s is waiting at Immingham Docks while the third three wagons are loaded under the hopper discharge unit. On arrival at Scunthorpe, the wagons were turned over and back over a large hopper, one wagon at a time, while remaining coupled to their neighbours, in an emptying operation that took no more than twenty-five minutes for the whole train.

It is not always easy taking pictures in bad weather, and fog is about the worst because light meters can be confused by the light scatter. I was disappointed that fog spoiled the view at Reading, but was able to obtain this rather ethereal shot of a high speed train passing through while a Southern Region 4CIG electric multiple unit stood at Platform 4, and a 117 class DMU awaited departure from the bay on the right. Do not ask why, but I rather like this photograph!

ABOVE: In 1975, BR attempted to re-enact the 1925 cavalcade at Shildon as a way of celebrating 150 years of railways in this country. One locomotive that I did not expect to see there, because it had previously stood on its plinth at Wantage Road station for what seemed like decades, was the Wantage Tramway 0-4-0 well tank *Shannon*, fully restored to working order and looking really sweet. Luckily, the field in which the Bournemouth Railway Club party had booked cheap standing places – 50pence each – had the sun behind the photographers, whereas the media team with their van (left background) were facing the wrong direction for the light!

RIGHT: On a visit to my parents in the Isle of Wight, I took the children to see the Isle of Wight Steam Railway based at the village of Havenstreet, though the station nameboards showed 'Haven Street' as two words. The Adams Class O2 0-4-4T W24 *Calbourne* had been restored to full working order in Southern Railway post-war lined-out malachite green and 'sunshine' lettering, and looked really smart. The large vertical pump at the left side of the smokebox pumps air for the train braking system. Unlike steam trains on other parts of the Southern Railway and Region, trains on the Isle of Wight were air braked on the Westinghouse system. This was a faster-acting brake than the standard vacuum type, and well suited to the stop-start nature of trains on the island, particularly on the Ryde to Ventnor run.

A holiday in Wales in 1976 enabled the family to see several of the narrow gauge railways there. Visiting the Talyllyn Railway, we witnessed a train from Towyn Wharf arriving at the then terminus at Abergynolwyn. The locomotive was one of the two original Fletcher-Jennings engines, 0-4-0T No 2 *Dolgoch*.

Less frequently visited, it seemed, was the Fairbourne Railway, situated just across the mouth of the Mawddach estuary from Barmouth, a short trip in a tourist motor boat. In this picture, the fifteen-inches gauge line is in full view of the magnificent Barmouth viaduct with its timber piers that many years later would succumb to being partially eaten away by sea worms, causing a long closure of the BR railway at this point. The Fairbourne Railway itself would be altered later to twelve-and-a-quarter inches gauge, but here it was still on the original gauge and a 2-4-2 tender engine named *Sîan* was pictured coasting towards the outer terminus. The railway had a second locomotive of this type named *Katie*, and was also running a 4-6-2 of more main line outline. Since its change of gauge, an interesting feature of the Fairbourne Railway has been that its locomotives are scaled-down replicas of well-known narrow gauge locomotives.

Our family move to Scotland in 1976 coincided with a change in the colour slide film I was using. I had been getting frustrated at the Agfa film's apparently increased contrast which had caused bleached-out skies and blocked shadows in contrasty conditions. I tried Kodachrome 200, and found it more even in its response to my normal methods of setting exposures. So, early on in Glasgow I tried it on a sunny day at Central station with pleasant results, such as this 1976 view of 87020 *North Briton* leaving with a train that included several new mark 3 coaches, bound for London Euston. There was still one mark 2 first class coach in the formation as well as the old mark 1 RUB that provided kitchen and buffet space, but these two vehicles, and the mark 1 BG van at the front, had bogies able to be hauled at up to 100mph. The mixture included vehicles with clasp brakes and disc brakes, which had different characteristics leading to frequent action of the mark 3s' wheel slide prevention equipment!

A4 pacific 60009 *Union of South Africa* was – and still is – a star performer on main line special trains. In the mid-1970s, it was based at a locked shed at Markinch. I photographed it leaving Leuchars, the former junction for the St Andrew's branch, heading north towards Dundee and Aberdeen. The 'modern' craze of enthusiasts for taking audio recordings is evident from the large microphone being held aloft out of the leading carriage window. I confess that my recorder was on the ground near me, the results being imperfect because of the gusty wind that was blowing at the time.

My friend Alan and I went to Polkemmet colliery near Edinburgh to watch the well-known double-heading that regularly took place with pairs of Barclay 0-6-0Ts climbing towards the exchange siding with trains of loaded coal wagons. Double-heading did not happen on this day, just the one 0-6-0T slogging slowly up the grade, its Giesl ejector chimney chuffing manfully but with ominous clanks from its bearings. This picture, taken on Kodachrome 200 on an overcast day, shows how on occasions an industrial scene could be almost completely colourless!

In 1977, Alan and I visited the remains of the Waterside system that served some NCB installations in Ayrshire. Barclay 0-6-0 side tank No. 17 was working alongside the washery at Waterside propelling a load of spoil tipper wagons uphill, which it would push for a few miles to a tip near the closed Minnivey mine. In the background is steam from the Giesel-fitted sister locomotive that was shunting the washery itself. The foreground track was the exchange siding where BR diesel locomotives would collect loaded wagons for onward distribution. This had once been a very busy industrial valley with many coal and ore trains feeding the ironworks at nearby Dalmellington. By the early 1980s, silence had descended on the area.

East Germany began to open up to tourists in the mid to late 1970s, so in summer 1978 Mary and I, leaving our children in the care of grandparents, travelled to Saalfeld to photograph steam-hauled trains on DR. My tendency to photograph anything that moved helped because there were many diesel-hauled trains around that had unfamiliar locomotive types at the front. This express accelerating towards the Gera line is headed by B-B diesel hydraulic 118.133, a DR equivalent of the West German V200 type. Indeed, the 118s were formerly classified V200 by DR. The locomotive depot on the left was hosting a large number of steam locomotives, mainly pacifics of Class 01^5, large 2-10-0s of Class 44, and some ex-Prussian 2-10-2Ts of Class 95, the latter being survivors of a former age long extinct in the West. When we left for the DDR, our West German friends saw us off from Frankfurt and were clearly very worried indeed that we would not be able come back. Thankfully we made it, though when we were about cross the DDR/BRD border at Probstzella our passports were taken away for twenty-five long minutes, presumably for detailed checking; the East German old-age pensioners who made up most of the other passengers looked at us sadly, until a smartly-uniformed official returned to our compartment, clicked his heels, and handed the newly-stamped passports to us. At that point, the diesel engine at the front erupted into action and our train was soon away to the West, and freedom.

I was delighted to see 'pre-grouping' Prussian 2-10-2Ts working around Saalfeld as I had never seen one in West Germany. This one, 95.0041, was pulling out of Saalfeld station with a service from the north heading towards stations in the Thüringerwald. Saalfeld departures faced steep climbs in two of the three directions in which trains left the station, only those heading towards Jena having easy gradients. The black smoke almost certainly came from the use of lignite coal, plentiful in East Germany and Poland. The driver had kept the engine's cylinder drain cocks open for the departure, causing a lot of cinders to be thrown up as the front of the engine passed my tape recorder! The double-deck carriages on the left were part of a standard eastern Europe type of fixed formation articulated set; the carriage articulations rode on six-wheeled bogies.

ABOVE: The last pit to use steam locomotives in Scotland was Bedlay colliery, east of Glasgow. Little Barclay 0-4-0ST 17 is just starting away from the washery with a train of 16ton wagons loaded with coal. It would firstly draw these slowly across a weighbridge, and then charge manfully uphill with the loaded train, reaching the exchange sidings where BR would remarshal the wagons and take them on to their destinations. The two-man NCB crew for this operation was a driver, who also fired the locomotive, and a shunter. They were loudly critical of British Rail who would meet them at the exchange sidings with a pair of Class 20 diesels and four people, a driver, shunter, wagon examiner and guard!

RIGHT: At around 2am on 4 January 1979, with Aberdeen shrouded in freezing snow, the final touches are applied to HST unit 254 015 being examined in the new Clayhills single-track depot. This photograph stretched my Rollei 35 camera to its limit, as well as my ability to hold it steady in low light conditions. With 100ASA Ilford FP4 film developed in Microdol, the exposure would have been in the order of 1/30th second at f/3.5. Thankfully the new depot lighting was of a high standard.

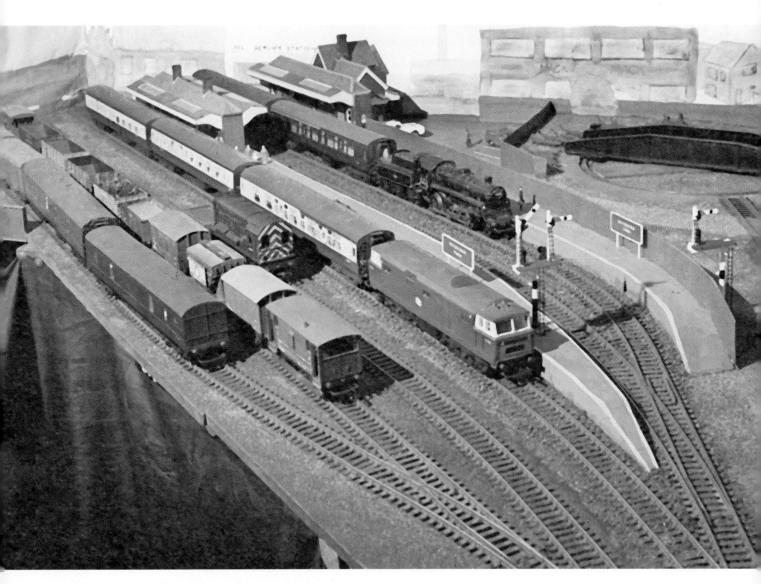

In order successfully to photograph my model railway in Doncaster, I borrowed a colleague with his Praktica single lens reflex camera. Using bounced flash, with FP4 film, the results were good enough for my small 00-scale layout to be published in the magazine *Railway Modeller* as its 'Railway of the month'. This picture shows the upper terminus called Weybourne Town, so named because it was supposedly somewhere between Weymouth and Bournemouth. This was years before I realised that there was a real place with that name on a heritage railway in north Norfolk! In the picture, a Hymek-headed departure is signalled that is bound for the Western Region. The layout fitted inside a box room of eight feet by five feet, and included a double-track main line with a second branch dipping down towards unseen – and non-existent – docks; quite a lot in a small space! In those impecunious days, one tried to keep costs as low as possible. The BR Class 4 2-6-0 is an Airfix plastic body kit on a very old Triang chassis (the driving wheels are too small); the Hymek diesel was in a model shop going for £2.50 as a non-runner – all that was needed was to adjust one motor brush spring and it worked well; the GUV van on the left is scratch-built in plastic card on a spare Hornby-Dublo mark 1 coach underframe. All still exist in 2017!

CHAPTER 5

THE 1980S – BR PROGRESS, UK AND CONTINENTAL RAILWAY PRESERVATION

If any one feature of railways featured strongly in the 1980s, apart from continued modernisation, it was the expansion and maturing of the railway preservation movement. This was as much apparent in Ireland and on the European continent as in the UK.

And if the 1970s had witnessed the nadir in the quality of my photography due to the replacement of FP3 film by FP4 and to my inability fully to embrace that and the changes in the make-up of colour slide films, so the 1980s were a decade of useful improvement for me. Ilford brought out its XP1 film, a 400ASA black-and-white film based on colour negative technology. When home-developed in Ilford's own specially constituted chemicals, the results were fine grain with superb tonal gradation. I became hooked on this and my black-and-white prints of that time were among my best. In the early 1990s, Ilford gave up selling its own chemicals and advised users of XP1 and its 'upgrade' XP2 to use the standard C41 colour negative film developer; I did not get such brilliant results from this, and eventually switched entirely to colour negative photography. But that change for the better is for the next chapter of this book.

An improvement in colour slides came when Agfa replaced its 64ASA CT18 emulsion with a new film, Agfachrome CT100. This new film was usefully faster, gave excellent colour renderings and had

significantly less grain than its forebear. So I switched back from Kodak to Agfa, and remained with CT100 until I stopped taking colour slides altogether.

The other change that helped to improve my photography was the purchase in 1985 of a Minolta X-300 SLR camera. I used this for black-and-white work, which was still my definitive medium for recording locomotive types and railway scenes. While its Minolta standard 50mm fixed lens was superb, I wanted a zoom lens, and picked a 70-150mm one from the Tamron range. This, too, proved to be excellent, giving me far more flexibility in the scenes I could compose. My Rollei 35 was confined to my static collection after fifteen years of use.

Even though the X-300 was marketed by Minolta as 'an entry level SLR', I was so impressed with its performance that I bought a second one in 1986. This was for colour slides, prompting the end of twenty-seven years of regular use of the trusty Voigtländer Vito IIa. Later, as I was taking a good number of general pictures when on holiday, including architectural scenes and townscapes, I also wanted a wider angle lens. A Tamron 28-70mm lens suited my purpose well, and gave me some extra compositional possibilities with railway scenes as well.

The 1980s began with the 'Liverpool & Manchester 150' celebrations at Rainhill, with a cavalcade and exhibition of railway locomotives and rolling stock. Other UK initiatives that decade were the series of garden festivals aimed at revitalising what were beginning to appear as failing cities. Liverpool was the first, followed by Stoke-on-Trent, Glasgow, Merthyr and Gateshead. Mary and I visited the first four, of which in my view Liverpool was the best, though Glasgow ran it a close second. All featured rail as a means of getting around the festival site. Liverpool's was a bold exercise in fifteen-inch gauge, having several gradients of up to 1 in 40 on a winding circuit. The donating railways responded by sending their strongest engines. The Romney, Hythe & Dymchurch Railway sent its 4-8-2 *Samson* and its tough German 4-6-2 *Black Prince*. The Ravenglass & Eskdale Railway provided the lovely old 0-8-2 *River Irt*, good at hill climbing, and the 2-6-2 diesel *Shelagh of Eskdale*. They were all given heavy trains to pull and the locomotives performed well. The festival site echoed with engine whistles for the duration of the summer! At Stoke, a fleet of immemorable railcars took riders up and down the hillside site. Glasgow had both a railway, with internal-combustion driven replicas of Stirling singles that looked okay, and a proper tramway using former Glasgow trams. I cannot remember how we got around the otherwise well-laid-out site near Merthyr. We did not get to the Gateshead festival.

In photographing the general railway scene, a career move from Glasgow to Manchester, followed by a year working in London and then finally settling in Derby, enabled me to explore unfamiliar routes and stations and to record the changes that BR brought in, often making better use of its rolling stock assets to reduce its costs. With our three children now forming a teenage group, more distant holidays were possible and we managed to get them to southern Portugal by train in 1986 and Yugoslavia by air

in 1988. I did break away from the latter and trekked by train across the continent from the Dover-Ostend ferry through Germany and Austria, followed by a slow journey through the Yugoslav republics of Slovenia, Croatia and Serbia, getting to the Montenegro resort in time to meet our family on their arrival.

Meanwhile, in the UK we travelled on many preserved railways including the Bo'ness & Kinneil Railway near Edinburgh, the Strathspey Railway, though my photographs of BR in the Highlands had much more impact, and in the North of England and the Midlands. It is a fact that visits to preserved railways, unless travelling on one's own unencumbered by family or friends, rarely give the opportunities to search out and sit quietly at ideal positions to photograph passing trains. Nonetheless, family comes first and one must use any opportunity to see a picture and grab it.

With my friend Nick Bartlett, I discovered the joys of the May weekend steam specials run by the Railway Preservation Society of Ireland. These have a two-day outing from Dublin as their core, but a programme of other trips and visits is fitted in over the days before and after the weekend. The two-day tour visits a destination distant from the capital, and usually finishes on the Sunday with an arrival at Belfast and a stock move, on which participants can ride, to the RPSI site at Whitehead. On the Saturday evening a 'banquet' is arranged and guests stay at a good quality hotel. Normally two steam locomotives find active employment during the tours and sometimes there is some fine running. I recall timing the old Great Northern 4-4-0 171 *Slieve Gullion* at a highly creditable 68mph on the main line from Cork to Dublin. There was a very audible, crackling roar from the engine's exhaust. Suddenly the sound stopped, and I asked innocently, 'Why has he shut off?' 'We've got to the top!' was the informed reply. I had had no idea we were actually running uphill at that significant speed!

On trips such as these it is often temping to lean out of the carriage window to take photographs of the engine at the front of the train, if the bend it is rounding is sharp enough to get a good view. I have tried this – note, not recommended as a health & safety activity – and am usually disappointed at the results. There are exceptions, such as when travelling on a slow narrow gauge train in a scenic area – I recently had some good results from the rear carriage of a train on the former forestry railway out of Moldoviţa in Romania. There is one such picture in the next chapter taken not so far from there but on a standard gauge roadside railway. This type of photography requires a steady hand, a fast shutter speed, and the ability to hold the camera away from any part of the carriage, otherwise the knocks that come from any rough riding will destroy any chance of a good photograph. It is equally difficult to get really good scenic pictures when aiming at passing scenery. How many times has one taken a nice mountain view, only to find a blurred telegraph pole or bush blocking part of the view? My solution in these circumstances is to set my camera on continuous repetition so that it takes a picture every second or so. That usually works, and with digital cameras it is easy afterwards to delete the unwanted or repetitious photographs. I did that when crossing from Romania on the Danube bridge on the approach to Ruse in Bulgaria; the bridge girders were getting in the way of a clear view of the river, but by taking about six shots at a fast interval, one was acceptable.

Then there is the scourge in modern trains of fixed windows with tinted glass. These have been with us since the DB launched its posh, air-conditioned Rheingold train in 1961. You cannot drop a window and lean out, so you try to take pictures through the glass. Beware of reflections! It is surprising how people just do not see the reflections in the window that the camera sees and will reproduce faithfully. The human brain just filters these reflections out, but the camera cannot. You have consciously to watch out for them, and find a camera position where reflections are at a minimum. I do not worry so much about the darker tones of an image that come through tinted glass. The final print or image can always be adjusted to take out any colour cast, and to brighten it up to a realistic contrast.

I have to admit that I am not much of a fan of main line steam trips in the UK. This may be because I travelled the length and breadth of our country behind steam when I was young. However, once or twice I have been persuaded to go out and photograph the occasional steam special; I can count the 1980s ones on one hand. I recall my wife's comment as we watched Mr Bulleid's 4-6-2 34092 *City of Wells* climbing the north ramp of the Settle & Carlisle line. 'What a beautiful locomotive!' she exclaimed as it chattered past. Coming from a Swindon-born lady, that was praise indeed! An hour or so later, after the train had stopped to water the locomotive from a tanker lorry at Dent, we were near the top of the climb. Nick and I were standing in a field as the rain came down, and Mary and our long-suffering children waited nearby in our rapidly steaming-up car. Soon *City of Wells* was heard approaching the summit near Ais Gill and someone commented, 'She's really going!' Indeed she was, hauling thirteen coaches at approaching 60mph with a volcanic exhaust and the steam sanders going flat out. What a wonderful sight! After that excitement, you cannot blame me and Nick that some of our photographs bear evidence of camera shake!

In the 1980s, steam specials over the Settle & Carlisle line were particularly popular because of the gradients and the striking scenery. Many of these trains ran under the title 'Cumbrian Mountain Express'. In 1983, an up-market version of this idea was the 'Cumbrian Mountain Pullman' formed partly of Metro-Cammell Pullman cars. On a wet and windy day, the Howarth-based 'West Country' 4-6-2 34092 *City of Wells* put out a superb performance, making a fine sight as it approached Ais Gill summit at approaching 60mph with thirteen coaches in tow. There was just a whisper of steam from a safety valve and the steam sanders were working flat out.

You could argue that we should have been using tripods. Mounting one's camera on a firm tripod holds it steady. All the photographer has then to do is to compose the picture in the viewfinder, cock the shutter, and fire the camera when the train reaches the desired spot. In reality I prefer not to carry my tripod on trips, wanting to travel light. I have occasionally used it, for example on commissioned work in depots or other dark scenes when a high quality result is needed. Otherwise, no. Anyway, my

picture of 34092 near Ais Gill was taken in such appalling light that I decided to move the camera to follow the engine's movement in an attempt to reduce any obvious blur in the photograph. I hope you like it!

On the subject of low-light photography, I once wrote an article about photographing Underground trains in London, in underground stations. With 400ASA film I could cope with the camera set at 1/60th at f/3.5, provided the oncoming train was not too close and was seen from a near head-on position; how much easier it is in today's digital age with the benefit of variable image speeds/ISO numbers! The same applies to photographing trains in stations and yards at night when the only light is from the station lighting. Often, illumination is worse than in underground stations and, in the absence of a handy tripod, I have sometimes leaned against, or held the camera against, a convenient upright. There are examples of this in this chapter.

There is one rule I must emphasise very strongly. No photographer must ever use flash when photographing a train where the photographer can be seen by the driver. Apart from the fact that flash is usually ineffective in railway contexts because of the distance between the camera and the subject, so it is pointless anyway, the real danger is of temporarily blinding the driver who may catch the full force of the flash in his or her eyes unexpectedly; this at a time when the driver is concentrating on stopping the train at the right place, or is preparing for departure. Some bodies such as London Underground have rules that prohibit flash, and quite rightly, too. But whether or not written rules are in place, flash has dangerous consequences for train drivers. The rule is – 'Do not use flash!'

I once wanted to use flash when I intended to photograph a South African electric locomotive that had coupled to our train during the night, and which would not be there when daylight came several hours later. What I did was to speak to the driver and ask if I could use flash to photograph his locomotive while it stood at the platform. He agreed, and kept out of the line of sight until I had finished. As Mr Punch would have said: 'That's the way to do it!'

Colour: Voigtländer Vito IIa 35mm camera [to 1986]
Black-and-white: Rollei 35 camera with 40mm lens [to 1985]
Then two Minolta X-300 35mm SLRs for colour and black-and-white, with additional Tamron 28-70mm and 70-150mm zoom lenses shared between them
On a horribly dull day in 1980, the Scottish Railway Preservation Society ran a tour using the former North British Railway 0-6-0 673 *Maude* piloting Gresley three-cylinder 4-4-0 246 *Morayshire*. The pair is seen crossing Larbert viaduct heading north on a roundabout tour that ended, for *Maude*, at Motherwell. Had the sun shone that morning, it would have been against the camera, so it is not always helpful!

NBR 0-6-0 673 stands at Motherwell depot at the end of its stint on the railtour in the previous picture. One or two bystanders were a distraction in the composition of this picture. This is the only photograph in the whole book that I will admit to modifying by crudely removing people in Adobe Photoshop Elements!

Facing the station throat at Glasgow Queen Street are two Scottish Region Class 47 Co-Cos. The nearest is 47712 *Lady Diana Spencer*, only recently reliveried and named. This was one of the twelve locomotives modified for push-pull operation with mark 3 coaches and mark 2f driving trailers for the fast, half-hourly service between Glasgow and Edinburgh. In the background is 47125 with early mark 2 stock on a service to Aberdeen. Queen Street station was photogenic from almost any angle. The dark walls date the picture to 1981, as they were stone-cleaned in the next year or so to relieve their blackness. The Inter-City trains to Aberdeen were converted to push-pull later, with three more 47s being converted to add to the 47/7 fleet.

To get mark 3 sleeping cars to Aberdeen, BR civil engineers had to increase lineside and platform clearances at several locations, including Dundee station. This picture was taken on the occasion of the first trial run in Scotland of a full train formation of these modern cars. Traction and rolling stock engineers are present as the train calls at Dundee in early 1981 on its way back to Craigentinny depot in Edinburgh. This was a lucky hand-held photograph on FP4 film making maximum use of the station lighting and home developed in Acutol. I am delighted that the platform starter bracket signal is so clear against the sky at dusk. The locomotive is a 47/4 equipped for electric train supply.

Railway life is not always straightforward! Someone has parked their Vauxhall Viva over the hatched area on Weymouth Quay and gone shopping. Along comes the Channel Islands boat train behind Bo-Bo 33101 which cannot get past the obstruction, at least not until the accompanying policeman has found a key that fits and has driven the errant car to a safer place. So, a ten-coach train has to wait, as does the ferry about 200 yards away, until this little excitement is over. No wonder the Weymouth Quay branch line is no longer used! This may not class as a pictorial photograph, but at the time it was newsworthy, and it is full of action of the human kind.

I was at Parkstone station photographing Class 33/1 diesels on push-pull trains in 1983, and was ready to go back to my friend's house when I espied this brilliant sunlight striking across the station's Up platform. So, when my train appeared, I had to take a photograph as it breasted the top of the first stretch of 1 in 60 up from Poole to call at the station. The diesel was propelling a 4TC trailer unit that would be attached at Bournemouth station to the back of the next electric service to London Waterloo. Using diesel push-pull trains in this way was an efficient method of working Weymouth trains almost seamlessly even though the third rail did not extend west of Branksome at that time. I stood in the shadow for this shot as, had the sun shone directly on the front of my lens there would have been a risk of flaring in the image from light rays refracted off the lens surface.

Living in the fine city of Glasgow, our family took several opportunities to explore Scotland on holiday. Twice we stayed at Abernethy and I found several locations near the Highland main line that could show a train as part of the scenery. This is an evening shot of the night sleeping car train from Inverness to London dropping down from Slochdt summit near Carrbridge, with the sun glinting off the mark 3 sleeping cars behind the erstwhile Class 47/4 Co-Co diesel. I regard this as good luck rather than good planning; it's a case of being in the right place at the right time and on the right day to catch the sun at its best angle.

When BR decided to build mark 3 sleeping cars for the London-Scotland overnight trains the Scottish Region faced a dilemma. It had no locomotives that could run on the line to Fort William that could deliver electric train supply (ets). Engineers at Aberdeen Ferryhill developed a cheap and local solution. They disconnected the traction motors of a redundant Class 25 Bo-Bo diesel electric and diverted the generator output to new ets connections at the locomotive ends. The Sulzer engine governor was pegged to hold the engine maximum speed at that which produced an output voltage correct for ets. Three such locomotives were converted, and given numbers from 97250 to 97252. They were known as ETHELs (Electric Train Heat Ex-Locomotives). In this 1983 view at Glasgow Queen Street, 37085 with 97252 coupled inside has just arrived from Fort William with that night's service to London. Eventually, when money became available, a group of 37s was modified to deliver ets, becoming Class 37/4, and the ETHELs were withdrawn.

Another steam special, this time heading west from the Settle direction towards Carnforth, is seen broadside near Clapham. The locomotive is former Somerset & Dorset Railway Class 7F 2-8-0 13809 performing competently as it whisks its train through the rain. After the initial success of these locomotives on the S&DJR, I am most surprised that the LMS, which designed and supplied these eleven useful 2-8-0s, never built any for itself, preferring instead to go on building the mediocre 4F 0-6-0s. History has never fully explained this apparent lack of ambition. Some photographers would have cut down the bushes by the lineside to get a clearer view of the engine. To keep the locomotive's image sharp, I moved the camera to parallel 13809, giving the background a little blur.

The idea of garden festivals was intended to kick-start development at run-down former industrial cities. Liverpool was the first, opening in 1984 for five months, and it was possibly the most ambitious. While the gardens were superb, bearing in mind that the land on which they were laid had been derelict two years before, a prominent and popular feature was the extensive light railway that was built to move people around the site. This was a fifteen-inch gauge railway looping the gardens with several gradients of up to 1 in 40, meaning that the locomotives would have to work hard to cope. All the locomotives selected were ideal for the purpose, being recognised individually as the strongest on their respective railways, the Romney, Hythe & Dymchurch and the Ravenglass & Eskdale, each of which provided two engines for the task. This picture shows R&ER 0-8-2 *River Irt* with nine bogie coaches in tow. What a pity that the whole railway was demolished after the festival had closed. It took twenty years before Liverpool got the gardens up to a fair standard again.

Sometimes, a railway photographer has to make the best of a bad job. On a wet day when the family visited the Keighley & Worth Valley Railway, for example, only the watery platform and some human action provide a bit of brightness to an otherwise dull scene. On my last visit to this 4¾ miles-long railway, the volunteers had cleaned and painted everything to the point that it was all so pristine as to be almost unbelievable!

By 1986, the 37/4s had enabled ScotRail to eliminate the last of BR's steam-heated trains, those on the Highland peripheral routes. At Kyle of Lochalsh, 37416 awaits the arrival of the ferry from Kyleakin, Isle of Skye, before departing for Inverness with the afternoon train. I particularly liked the BR large-logo livery which was a bold attempt to make BR appear more modern and forward-looking. The excellent optical performance of the Minolta 50mm standard lens is evident, as is the better quality of Agfa's colour slide film following the upgrade from CT18 (18DIN speed, 64ASA) to CT100 (100ASA, nowadays called ISO100).

During 1985-86 I was attached to a British Railways Board team in London studying and making recommendations to improve traction and rolling stock downtimes and reduce costs at main works and depots. I had spare time in the evenings to explore the railways around London. I wanted to photograph the existing scene as well as new developments. This view at Willesden Junction Low Level meets both targets. A Class 501 EMU arrives on a Euston to Watford Junction service while a former SR-style two-car Class 416 unit calls at the High Level platforms when working on the North London line from Richmond to North Woolwich, a route newly extended at the east end following the demise of the Broad Street terminus. The 416s worked temporarily on that route until modern Class 313 electrics were drafted in. In this photograph, I like the criss-crossing of strong lines at obtuse angles that seem to focus the eye on the oncoming EMU.

I wanted to photograph trains coming off Marple viaduct in Cheshire, a scene I saw in a book during steam days. My visit in 1986 found that the view I had in mind of the west end of the viaduct had become totally obscured by the growth of young trees. I half-heartedly took a few pictures of the side of the viaduct, but this one was a piece of sheer good luck. Just as the most unexciting train came across the viaduct, a Pacer DMU, these canoeists crossed the parallel aqueduct, making the picture far more interesting. One needs something like this when trying to lift the limited impact of diesel and electric train pictures! The footpath and stone wall on the right help to lead the eye into the picture.

A District Line train of D78 stock arrives at Mansion House on a winter's evening heading eventually to Ealing Broadway. I enjoyed trying to get pictures of London's Underground away from the broad daylight sections, even though light was limited underground and there were train movements to be caught without blurring. A near head-on position can enable a moving train to appear sharp at a relatively slow shutter speed, such as here, though the actions of passengers on the platforms are not always so helpful.

Living now at Derby, I explored with some friends the area around the Peak District limestone quarries. This is an important source of freight traffic for our railways. In this 1987 shot, 37681 and 37682 in multiple back into a siding at Hindlow while making up a loaded train of limestone hopper wagons. The oblique angle of the sun is not conventional, but it gives this picture some contrast while emphasising the exhausts of the locomotives. Also, my aim is normally to have the main subject on the intersection of two thirds, not in the middle of an image as here, but this works in this case because the curve of the line of foreground 16ton mineral wagons focuses the eye on the locomotives.

On another occasion in 1987, we were waiting just uphill from Tunstead quarry in Derbyshire for a very late-running steam special when this unusual combination came along. 'Peak' 1Co-Co1 45034 was piloting Co-Co 47258 on a train of loaded four-wheeled covered hoppers as the sun glimmered briefly. The bracket signal on the left, a standard LMS/BR tubular post type, helps to frame the picture, and again disproves the intersection of two thirds rule! Tunstead's better-known traffic was the regular flow of limestone to Northwich which was carried in ICI-branded bogie hopper wagons, some of which dated to pre-war years.

In Austria in 1987 I fell in love again. Unusually, it was with a steam locomotive. I was touring with friends Alan Wild and Nick Bartlett and we were having a day out on a steam special from Vienna as part of Austria's '*Eisenbahn* 150' celebrations. The locomotive was Mr Gölsdorf's four-cylinder compound 2-6-4 express engine 310.23. We disembarked for a break at Gänserndorf, and I sat for ten minutes transfixed by this beautiful vision of art and science in steel. Indeed, when the train pulled away, I almost missed it! I realise this shape is not everyone's cup of tea, but I really do like it.

During the same tour, Nick, Alan and I went crocodile hunting in the Alps. We found this one, which arrived at Thusis on the Rhätische Bahn in south-east Switzerland hauling a pick-up freight. These metre-gauge C-C 'crocodiles' have reduced to just two heritage examples now, but they are a classic electric locomotive design that was introduced in 1925 and survived in traffic for nearly seventy years. The RhB added a carriage to the front of this train, which was marked 'G' for *Guterzug* (goods train) in the timetable. We travelled in that carriage all the way up the tortuous Albula Valley line to Samedan, shunting at wayside stations as required, and being passed and overtaken there by the hourly expresses on this fascinating and well-run metre-gauge railway. Lovely!

At Ryde Pier Head in 1987, a former London Transport Piccadilly Line train leaves for Shanklin with passengers off the ferry from Portsmouth Harbour. During the electrification works, tracks in Ryde tunnel were raised to accommodate buried services, and small loading gauge trains became necessary, for which the redundant Underground trains were ideal. This electrification was introduced in 1966 at minimum cost. These trains were among the first on the Southern Region of BR to receive the all-over standard rail blue livery. These ancient units, later looking smarter in blue-and-grey, were eventually replaced at the end of the 1980s by LT 1938 stock, a year with which I can identify, being my birth year. The church spire on the left horizon marks All Saints' church where I was baptised. The 1938 ex-tube stock still runs on this service today, and is the oldest in the country operating on a main line railway.

Cork Kent station, the former Glanmire Road, sits on a sharp curve just outside a steeply graded tunnel. In the days when the railways of Ireland were still dominated by locomotive haulage of long-distance passenger trains, the station had a prominent run-round loop to the south of the train shed. General Motors Co-Co diesel electric 071 is using this loop in summer 1988 to reposition itself after arrival with the 10.30am from Dublin, a train formed of fairly new mark 3 coaches, most of which were built at Inchicore Works, Dublin. These 124 vehicles were the first mark 3s in the British Isles to have automatic swing plug doors and were liveried in light tan, black and white.

Nick and I were visiting Ireland to take part in the 1988 weekend tour organised by the Railway Preservation Society of Ireland. This started from Dublin Heuston with ex-LMS (Northern Counties Committee) Class WT 2-6-4T No 4 hauling the train bunker first, with some very fast running as far as Ballybrophy where the train reversed. The train then traversed the less-well-used section via Nenagh to Limerick, this section including two run-pasts for photographers. At Birdhill the train passes a splendid set of CIÉ semaphore signals, all front faces being decked in luminous red, including the fishtailed distant arm on the right. Now, nearly thirty years later, nearly all semaphore signals in Ireland have gone.

A feature of the RPSI May weekend tours is the convivial atmosphere. On the 1988 tour, the buffet car crew reported the sale of one barrel each of bitter and lager beers and thirteen of Guinness! During a run-past on the then freight-only stretch between Ennis and Athenry two members of the Belfast Rowing Club – or so we were led to believe – enjoyed some up-market drinks while taking a walk on the ballast while the buffet car attendant looked on!

On the Monday following the tour, which had terminated at Belfast on the Sunday evening, it was necessary to return the coaching stock to its base at Whitehead on the Larne line. Until the new Dargan bridge would be opened across the River Lagan in Belfast in 1992, it was necessary to make a detour and take the stock from Belfast Central via Lisburn and the ex-GNR(I) branch through Crumlin to Antrim before going to Whitehead. The RPSI made this an additional tour day for anyone who wished to travel, and extended it to the seaside resort of Portrush using the superbly-restored Class V 4-4-0 compound 85 *Merlin* that had been built by Beyer Peacock in 1932. This former Great Northern Railway (Ireland) express engine is seen on the climb out of Portrush passing Dhu Varren halt. Its support coach is a classic ex-Great Southern & Western Railway twelve-wheeled clerestory tri-composite brake vehicle. The signal in the background is one of the very last operational somersault signals to survive in the UK, due to have been replaced by modern signals during 2016.

How do you make pictures of electric locomotives interesting? In this case, by including five assorted sidings full of coal hopper wagons with English Electric Bo-Bo No 15 shunting another rake, this view does show the locomotive doing what it was designed to do. The low-height cab enabled the locomotive to fit within the steeply-graded tunnel that linked the sidings here on the Westoe colliery system near South Shields with the staithes at Harton on the Tyne estuary. Again, I have broken my intersection of two thirds rule, but in this case it works.

No 15 has arrived at the staithes, and is reversing its train round the circle to bring the loaded hopper wagons over the unloading bunkers. During my visit in 1988, I was assured confidently by local management that the railway would remain open for a decade or more; however, this unique system regrettably ceased operating in 1993.

In late spring 1988, British Rail London Midland Region and Danish State Railways (DSB) ran a series of exchange visits between supervisors and staff from Willesden locomotive maintenance depot and that at Copenhagen. The idea was to learn from each other and to bring home useful practices. This locomotive washing shed was one idea that was not imported to the UK. DSB's early Class Mx A1A-A1A General Motors diesel electric 1001 was in the plant, not only getting a body wash but also a high-pressure scourge of its underparts. The enclosed shed paid homage to the much more severe winters in Denmark. In London, frozen locomotive washing machines are only a problem in the relatively few days of freezing winter weather.

During a visit to the Severn Valley Railway, I saw that Ivatt 2-6-0 43106 was sparklingly clean and facing out from the shed towards the bright outdoor light. I could not resist taking its portrait. Depot visits such as this on heritage railways are nowadays less easy to achieve, probably correctly, as managements tighten up their approaches to visitor behaviour and safety.

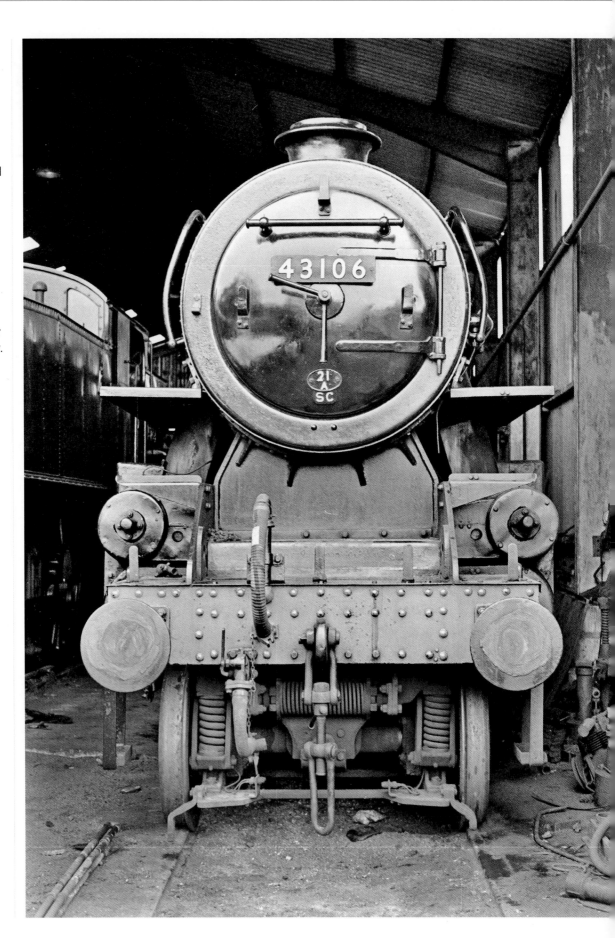

For two weeks in late 1988, I had to chair jointly with a colleague, Noel Broadbent, a large meeting of
management and staff representatives and their unions to consult on the reorganisation that would be a
step towards removing the regional level of management altogether, and of the London Midland Region of
BR in particular. The meeting was held in a large hotel on the sea front road at Blackpool. I was able to get
some light relief from this demanding task during midday and evening breaks by seeking out the famous
Blackpool trams that lumbered along the sea front. This view shows one of the double-deck 'balloon' cars
trundling towards the famous tower. The curves of the foreground tracks help to envelop the image of
the tram itself and act as a partial frame. This tram system has changed significantly in the twenty-first
century. Modern trams have replaced the old ones for regular daily transport. Examples of the older trams
are still deployed during holiday times and festivals.

In summer 1989, Alan Wild, Nick, Mary and I revisited Switzerland to attend the Rhätische Bahn's centenary celebrations, a whole weekend of playing trains on the line through Davos. Towards the end of the Sunday, we noticed a special train to Landquart being advertised that was not in the timetable. This turned out to be a stock move, happily with the bar car still open! The ten-coach train was worked by two of the three steam locomotives that had taken part in the events. Seen during the halt at Seneus, the pilot locomotive is 2-6-0T No 1 *Rhätia*, and the train engine is 2-8-0 107. The driver of the tender engine checks moving parts, while his oil can rests on the running plate above. Normally I like to have some visual stop in the railway photograph to prevent the eye wandering away from the subject. In this case, the drifting steam acts as a frame for the leading engine and I suggest that the two locomotives thus have sufficient impact to hold one's attention.

The same tour took us to Czechoslovakia, to Brno to see the 'Czech 150' celebrations. A very comprehensive set of exhibitions and special trains centred on Brno and Břeclav, and made it a worth-while week. Brno shed was open to visitors, something quite unusual in the eastern bloc at that time, and that is where the steam locomotives that had performed in that day's cavalcade returned for servicing that evening. One was this beautiful 4-8-2 express passenger locomotive 498.022. I included the bare foreground area in the wide-angle shot because I think it helps to draw the eye towards the magnificent blue engine. A noted authority on overseas locomotives wrote that the post-war Czech steam locomotive designs were probably the most advanced in the world. The dark sky presages a storm that arrived soon after I took this photograph. Mary and I were soaked through in the ensuing rainstorm, but it was worth it!

British Rail's high speed diesel trains, the HSTs, are world-beaters still after forty years of operation. The InterCity livery that they wore during the late 1980s and 1990s was among the best for that iconic fleet. This one is pictured arriving at Cheltenham on a Bristol to Newcastle service in 1989. I used a low angle for this shot deliberately to give the train a bit of 'bulk'. These are the trains that saved InterCity, and with it British Rail. When they were introduced, their operating speed of 125mph was just 10mph slower than the top speed of the first Japanese Shinkansen 'bullet trains', though developed versions of the latter have since reached 186mph (300kph) or more. An HST still holds the world speed record for a diesel train, however, 148mph.

As the East Coast Main Line electrification came to fruition I made attempts to photograph the impressive new IC225 trains, trying to portray the impact they would have on the performance on that key railway. This view at Leeds in 1989 shows 91004 in profile, bringing out its rakish lines. The slope of the cab front is repeated exactly by the angle of the white stripe behind the cab and countered by the italic slope of the InterCity motif. From an engineering viewpoint, these locomotives are innovative in the way that the body-hung traction motors reduce unsprung weight, and yet occupy much of the space they would if bogie mounted. They drive the wheels through telescopic cardan shafts and bevel gearboxes. Clever.

CHAPTER 6

THE 1990S – TOWARDS PRIVATISATION, THE WIDER SEARCH FOR WORKING STEAM

As people get older, subtle changes appear in the way they cope with their affairs and hobbies. In my case, in the 1990s, I detected a drop in the accuracy of the exposures I was giving colour slides. Agfachrome CT100 slide film had an improved emulsion which gave excellent colours and fine grain, but I found myself sometimes with several groups of slides either over- or under-exposed.

It was becoming clear that colour negative technology had advanced to the point that colour prints were affordable, and magazine editors were beginning to accept colour prints as well as slides for reproduction. Colour negatives offered a medium where minor exposure errors could be corrected during printing. Thus, I sought out some advice as to what were the two best colour negative films for colour accuracy and image quality. I asked a photographic laboratory in Nottingham who had done some excellent prints from slides for me; I also asked the same question of the manager of our local Jessops shop in Derby. Both, to my surprise, gave exactly the same answer: the best 35mm colour negative film for image quality and colour rendering was Fuji Reala 100, with Kodak Gold 200 as an excellent runner-up. That made my choice easy. I would try Fuji Reala 100, which I first did just before my wife arranged

for us a secret holiday to mark my sixtieth birthday; this turned out to be a Jules Verne trip to South Africa and Zimbabwe which included a few days on the 'Union Limited' train between Cape Town and Oudtshoorn, largely with steam haulage.

After I had sent a selection of pictures of our South African journeys to the magazine *Today's Railways*, the editor David Haydock rang me up and asked what film I was using – he was amazed at the print quality! I had had the Reala 100 film developed and printed by Jessops using their Gold standard print service, something I continued to use until a few years later when its quality began to drop off – but that is another decade in another chapter.

For a railway manager and railway photographer in the UK, the 1990s were ten years of more-or-less continuous change in that privatisation of British Rail was first mooted, and then implemented. By the end of the decade we were being confronted with new train liveries, some of them very attractive, and our railways suddenly became colourful, possibly as colourful as they had been before the 1923 grouping. This gave photographers new opportunities for varied compositions, perhaps improving on the well-established dilemma of how to make photographs of diesel and electric trains interesting.

The UK steam scene was also getting better as heritage railways became firmly established as successful businesses, a long way forward from the original theme of operation by enthusiastic amateurs, without whom, of course, the heritage railway movement would not have got off the ground. Also, towards the end of the decade, private companies began to assume the role of train operating companies on the national network. This enabled them to advertise steam and other special trains to different markets, and in turn to give lineside photographers plenty of scope to indulge, if this was their scene. Here I must confess that, having spent the first three decades of my life travelling around the UK on steam-hauled trains, I am less excited about main line steam specials today than are many photographers for whom it is their life's passion.

On the other hand, the prosperity that had gradually crept up on us in the UK was enabling many more people to travel abroad, particularly by air. In 1994, the Channel Tunnel opened, with the Eurostar trains making possible fast journeys to and from Paris and Brussels that were not influenced by rough seas or turbulent air. I found these enormously long high speed trains very photogenic, looking great as they swept through the centre tracks at Ashford, for example, or past suburban stations such as Wandsworth Road. Yes, the UK still did not have its own high speed railway. That would come in stages in the next two decades. Nonetheless, my friends and I enjoyed many trips seeking out different railways on the continent, always using rail as our means of travelling around.

Mary and I also preferred to travel long distances by train on holiday if we could. Thus, in May 1990, we travelled to Romania on a mission just five months after that country's revolution, joining the real 'Orient Express' in Paris and witnessing the presence of a few steam locomotives in Romania still engaged in shunting and freight transfer work, particularly around Arad and Ploieşti. Most of the remaining working engines were 0-10-0s of the Prussian type G.10, which had been built in Romania for CFR alongside lots of P.8 passenger engines. Wanting to visit that challenging country again in the autumn, on holiday this time, we made our twenty-fifth wedding anniversary journey to Venice on the 'Venice Simplon-Orient-Express', and then travelled via Yugoslavia to Romania. This time we routed ourselves via Timişoara to the capital, Bucharest – and met some teenage girls from a children's home on the train. One of these girls became our adopted daughter in 1992. This was indeed a life-changing train journey for us and for her. That would not have happened had we travelled by air!

When I retired from full time work early in 1996, I decided to take off alone for a couple of weeks and see how far south I could get by train. An early Eurostar got me from Ashford to Paris and I was soon heading into the middle of France on an unfamiliar route, via Clermont Ferrand. I overnighted in Nevers, crossed the border into Spain at Port Bou, and sat in an EMU heading for Barcelona. I diverted at Gerona because the old city looked so fascinating, and it proved to be delightful. Thus, I only saw the railway at Barcelona from underneath, in tunnels, as I changed trains at Barcelona Sants and headed for Zaragoza in the first Talgo train I had ridden in. Next morning, I met a resident engineer who had promised me a look round CAF's carriage-building works. I was impressed at the quality of CAF's work, especially the firm's careful storage of sheet steel in dry conditions to prevent the onset of corrosion. Equally impressive was the corrosion resistant coating that CAF sprayed on the body frame members of the first two carriages for Heathrow Express, which the firm was building with Siemens. The Hex cars looked small when compared with the 5ft 6in gauge suburban EMU coaches that CAF was building for the Spanish railways RENFE in the same workshop. My trip continued by express EMU to Madrid, and then a sleeping car train to Algeciras, from where I boarded a ferry for the two-hour crossing to Tangier in Morocco, with a day's delay because of rough seas in the Straits of Gibraltar. I used that delay to make a bus trip into Gibraltar, possibly the most disappointing place I have ever visited on tour. Eventually, I ended up in the fascinating city of Marrakesh, which was as far south as the Moroccan railway went, the last few hundred miles being in comfortable, air-conditioned stock with modern electric locomotive haulage. Morocco is one of the only three countries where I have ever been really sad at leaving, the others being Portugal and Romania.

After my retirement, my travels with Mary ventured further afield. We tried one of the classic trips across America by rail, starting in New York and reaching the west coast, with excursions including to the Grand Canyon. Again, I learned that when one travels by rail the opportunities for creative photography are limited by the schedule and the fact that one cannot normally reach the best lineside positions to photograph passing trains. The South African tour in 1998 proved to be an exception to this rule. The 'Union Limited's' train manager had the practice of watching his arriving guests at Cape Town station, and noting how many, if any, walked forward to look at the magnificent Class 25NC 4-8-4 at the front before the train started away. In the case of our tour, he was happy that there were enough enthusiasts on the train to justify arranging several lineside run-pasts, the first being in a particularly spectacular location, the exit from Tunnel 5 on the

Montague Pass just east of George. He herded everybody from the train who was fit enough to climb in and out of the carriages to stand on a small bluff near the trackside with a good view of the tunnel mouth. Then the train backed away into and beyond the tunnel. When it restarted, we were treated to the splendid sight of a Class 19D 4-8-2 piloting a GMAM Garratt 4-8-2+2-8-4 blasting their way uphill. Who needs bright sunshine with a picture opportunity like this?

The South African tour was the last occasion I used black-and-white film. The quality of the colour prints that Jessops was providing from my Fuji Reala 100 negative film was consistently superior to that of my home printing efforts, a reversal of my previous situation in which I pursued home developing and printing to keep my black-and-white quality up. Also, I had realised that using 100ASA colour film was okay for most situations, but there were occasions when light levels were too low for reliable photography of moving trains. I needed a colour film that was rated at 400ASA. So, having two identical Minolta X-300 cameras, it became sensible to use one for 100ASA Reala film, and one for Fuji's Superia 400 for poorer lighting conditions. This combination suited me well from 1998 until when I abandoned using film completely in 2004.

I also began choosing less popular times of the year for some trips. For example, a rail tour of Switzerland with my friend, Alan Wild, in February 1998, took me to a winter wonderland that I have never forgotten! I had experienced in sunny summers the superb metre gauge railway in the south-east, the Rhätische Bahn, but never in the snow. I decided to seek out and photograph the world-famous Landwasser viaduct, the one that takes the railway across a narrow valley, at the end of which the railway plunges straight into a tunnel in a vertical rock face. As I walked along the valley floor

I realised that, apart from the man who lived in a small chalet half way to the viaduct, I was the only human being in the valley! This came home to me as I scrambled up a snow-covered bank to reach the footpath I had missed earlier in the walk – if I fell I would not be found for weeks. Up on the correct path, I reached the vantage point that overlooks the viaduct. After about an hour at this striking location, while wondering how the RhB managed to cram so many trains into a single track main line in such a wild place, I was suddenly afflicted by vertigo, something quite alien to me. I had to crawl away from my vantage point. That has never happened again.

Readers will have noted that most of these trips did not involve chasing after steam locomotives. However, I was concerned to see some real live steam still working in odd corners of the world, doing what it was designed to do in a commercial way. My travels began to head even further afield, but most of this was from the year 2000 onwards, covered in the next chapter of this book.

In the UK, I was busy writing articles and railway books for different publishers. One book series was on train liveries from BR days and into privatisation. This gave me the impetus to travel around the country seeking out train colours local to different areas as well as finding the best way of illustrating the individual livery details.

For the BR era liveries, my own collection of pictures was helpful generally, but I had not previously homed in on smaller details such as nameplates, numberplates, cabside lining arrangements and unusual lettering styles such as those used initially when BR was formed in 1948. Thankfully, some of the heritage railways had locomotives running on them that exhibited these styles. I recall a visit to Bridgnorth depot on the Severn Valley Railway where

a 'Hall' class 4-6-0 was coupled to a Hawksworth tender that had BRITISH RAILWAYS painted in the former GWR style shaded lettering, a very useful example. The Midland Railway Centre at Butterley, not far from my home in Derby, was also a source of useful livery details, as was the Mid-Hants Railway which was running 34105 *Swanage* with a cut-down tender; the lining on the tender and cabsides was BR's orange-and-black spaced out in GWR style, correctly, and the long stripes on the air-smoothed casing were in the unique style adopted for Bulleid pacifics by BR from 1949, with the orange lines adjacent to and not spaced out from the black.

It was when I was photographing livery details on Great North Eastern Railway IC225 trains at Newcastle that I noticed that some were running with their GNER logos in white and not in the original gold colour. If you do not look closely at the detail you can miss this sort of thing! Thankfully, the style quickly reverted to gold, so the white lettering was a passing phase that I might have missed. Also, it was on the same photo tour that I noticed for the first time that the GNER badge on the carriage sides was a splendid brass plate on the HSTs, but applied in vinyl on the mark 4s. The latter looked so realistic that I had not noticed until then!

The use of vinyl to change train liveries quickly was a new thing in the late 1990s, but it certainly allowed the new franchisees to bring out some bold styles. Its only downside was that it made it easier and cheaper to apply temporary advertising liveries. I do not deliberately photograph these, and have been very disappointed that railways such as the Rhätische Bahn have covered all their new Bo-Bo electric locomotives with these usually garish schemes. If an advertising livery gets into this book, it will be because the photograph has some other redeeming feature!

In the 1990s, the heritage railway movement was becoming mature and the larger such railways were tending to be run like businesses in their own right. The early emphasis on 'volunteer-led' had given way to professional, business-like management that could be seen as akin to the entertainment and tourist industries. Money that these railways had earned began to flow and attracted new forms of investment. Facilities at stations were being upgraded and added to, locomotives and rolling stock were sent away for professional overhauls or even dealt with in-house by a qualified staff team. Some more adventurous railways managed to get free work done on their land by the military as training exercises, or by railway plant suppliers to demonstrate their wares, for example by getting a ballast tamper manufacturer to test its equipment by laying and tamping the ballast on the heritage railway's main line.

Photographing these heritage railways took on a new tack in that modern safety rules became evident. Photographers wanting good lineside positions had to apply for permits, and to wear high-visibility clothing, much to the chagrin of others outside the fences who did not want orange vests in their pictures of heritage trains! Access to some locomotive depots was restricted or banned. Nonetheless, these railways have proved to be good locations for railway photographers as they are not that demanding in technique, their trains never moving very fast, and most have some good landscape locations around them from which to photograph trains. Photographs taken of such railways are characteristically better than many we see of main line steam specials. As I have written earlier, fast-moving trains are often less photogenic than slow-moving ones.

Colour and black-and-white: Two Minolta X-300 35mm SLRs
One result of BR's limited and piecemeal electrification was and is the necessity of using diesel trains in electrified areas to maintain through connections. On 12 December 1992, a Cross-Country HST starts away from Bournemouth with the 14:17 'Pines Express' for Manchester. The exhaust from its Paxman Valenta engine is making its mark in the station atmosphere. This diesel will run along lines electrified at 750V dc third rail and 25kV AC overhead for much of its long journey. A five-car Class 442 EMU in the background has its multiple unit connections prepared for its next duty; more modern units than these 1980s ones have fully automatic couplers that include all air and electrical inter-unit connections.

An electric locomotive hauled container train passes southbound near Berkhamstead on the West Coast Main Line, said to be Britain's busiest main line. The locomotive is Bo-Bo electric 90142 and the date 7 September 1991. The colour slides I was taking around this time were on Agfachrome 100 film, which gave far better results that the same company's former CT18 slide film; I was getting finer grain, sharper resolution and better colour rendering.

A feature of Crich Tramway Village is this splendid Victorian pedestrian bridge, under which is approaching the very popular open tram 45 from Southampton. The tram has a unique sign on the top deck imploring passengers not to touch the overhead wire as it passes under the Bargate, a low and ancient gate through the city wall in Southampton! The tram tracks in the picture are gauntleted to pass through the bridge, that is they overlap each other for a few yards. Happily, the wire under this bridge is high enough not to be a threat to top-deck passengers!

This was 'Sheffield's last tram' according to the painted message on the ends of four-wheeled tram 510. It stands at the outer terminus at Crich Tramway Museum in Derbyshire, awaiting its return trip in summer 1990. Nowadays we are supposed to call the museum Crich Tramway Village. This reflects the efforts put in by the organisation to add buildings of Victorian aspect to form an attractive group around the main terminus, including a rather splendid pub called the Red Lion, a prominent feature of which is its glazed tile frontage. However, the largest building in the complex is the tram museum shed itself, which houses part of a very extensive collection, well worth a visit if you are in the area. Indeed, Crich Tramway Village is well worth travelling a long way to see.

At the new Docklands Light Railway station at Canary Wharf in 1990, one of the second batch of vehicles, No. 16, arrives with a working from Tower Hill to Island Gardens. These early vehicles were later sold to Essen in Germany and modified for use as street trams. For this they had to have drivers' positions fitted because, like all vehicles on the DLR, they had operated automatically without drivers, though a DLR staff member was present in the car to assist passengers and check tickets.

In the picturesque Bucovina province in northern Romania, the branch line to Moldovița peeled off at Vama, on the main line from Suceava to Cluj, and took the form of a standard gauge roadside tramway. Moldovița is now a tourist village with an attractive monastery as well as a narrow gauge steam railway reborn out of a former forestry line. Regrettably, the CFR branch line was closed before the tourist boom took off, otherwise it could have been an added tourist attraction in the area. This view in 1993 shows the Vama-bound train with a Class 80 Sulzer diesel hydraulic B-B at its head passing typical Romanian traffic – a horse and cart and a communist-era Dacia car based on the old Renault 12. The somewhat relaxed atmosphere in that region is illustrated by one carriage door swinging wide open, of no concern to anyone! The dull, rainy weather that day muted the colours, and this picture, while taken as a colour slide, perhaps has more impact in monochrome, an easy conversion in Photoshop Elements.

Most main lines in Romania were electrified in communist times, and CFR obtained over 800 excellent Co-Co electric locomotives based on a design by ASEA in Sweden, though the majority were built in Romania. 40-0843 leaves Simeria with the 'Pannonia Express' from Bucharest to Budapest which includes sleeping cars for the long, slow journey. After taking this picture, Alan and I were arrested by the station police. Apparently, it was illegal in Romania to photograph railway installations such as yards and stations. We obligingly paid up our fines of 700 lei each, amounting to little more than 56pence each in UK currency at the time! We checked whether trains could be photographed legally in the countryside, and the answer was, 'Yes.'

In the north of the former DDR is the island of Rügen which boats a 750mm gauge steam railway. At Posewald station, 2-10-2T 99.748 waits with its train from Puttbus to Gören while 0-8-0T 52M approaches with an Up train. This was 1993, only four years since the border was removed between the two Germanys, and the rolling stock still bears the designation DR. Nonetheless, the railway had already made the switch from being a local common carrier to a tourist railway.

Mary and I visited friends in southern Norway for New Year 1993/1994. On 29 December 1993, I took to the trains for a day visit to Oslo, first travelling from Skien to Nordagutu, where I changed into a main line Stavanger-Oslo service. These electric railcars at Nordagutu are on the Skien-Notodden service, passing at around 11:00, as daylight gains hold. By 14:30 it was already getting dark again.

The interior of the main terminus station at Antwerp in Belgium is architecturally impressive. In 1993, this SNCB two-car EMU had arrived from Liège Guillemains, a stopping train journey of over two hours, and it had just six minutes at Antwerp before beginning its return journey. Such a sharp operating schedule demands good timekeeping, even though the EMU must make other cross-platform connections en route. This station has been substantially rebuilt recently to accommodate the main line and the new high speed railway at lower levels; there are now three levels of platforms here.

On one of my rare visits to photograph trains on a heritage railway, some friends and I looked in on the Severn Valley Railway in spring 1994. Here, GWR 2-6-0 7325 has a correct rake of former Great Western Railway stock coaches in tow as it heads from Kidderminster towards Bridgnorth. The coaches are mostly in pre-1948 GWR brown-and-cream colours, but the locomotive's livery is actually post-1956 British Railways green, though that was based on the GWR colours. This railway makes an effort to put together rakes of carriages of a common railway of origin and livery, though it is not always possible to provide a matching locomotive.

My wife's favourite Swiss village is Kandersteg, high up on the original Lötschberg railway, a delightful location from which several long Alpine walks strike out. Back in 1994 it was not open-air walking weather when brown-coloured Bern Lötschberg Simplon Bahn (BLS) Class Re4/4 Bo-Bo 170 arrived with one of the southbound hourly inter-city trains. Indeed, I was grateful for the cover provided by the end of the platform awning! Modern cameras do not take kindly to use during downpours such as this one; the electronics can fail if the camera gets wet.

Two Eurostar high speed trains line up for departure from Waterloo International station on 14 October 1994, the year the Channel Tunnel opened. Four of the major infrastructure projects associated with the introduction of cross-Channel train travel have proved to be 'white elephants'. Two thankfully, after years of non-use, are finding new potential. The International platforms at Waterloo station are just now being converted for suburban train use, ten years after the trains' UK terminus transferred to St Pancras after when they have had very little use. The Eurostar depot at North Pole also lost its work when the trains moved to St Pancras, because a new depot was built for them at Temple Mills near Stratford, east London. North Pole is being resuscitated now to be a Hitachi depot for GW electric express trains. The viaduct that curved away from the Windsor lines to cross near Stewarts Lane, so that Eurostars could get from the Waterloo lines to those heading towards Folkestone, now stands forlorn and visually abandoned. The link at Fawkham Junction that took Eurostar trains from the main line near Swanley over to HS1 is now out of use. Anyone who took photographs of these expensive monuments to changes in policy has history in his or her collection.

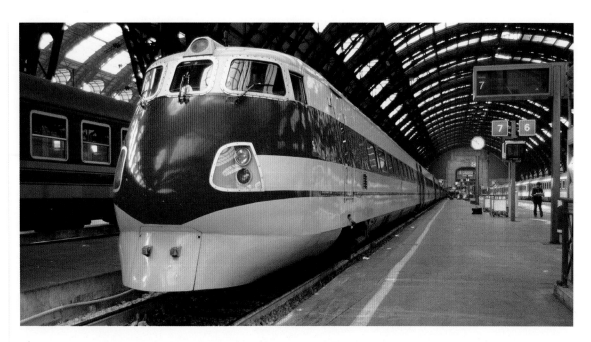

This old Class 450 'Pendolino', one of the first production series of Italian tilting trains, had arrived at Milan Central and I simply had to grab a photograph of it before the type eventually disappeared from main line services. Even in April 1994, the type was no longer on the fastest north-south services but was working on winding routes across the Appenines. I could have used Photoshop to paint out the bits of litter on the platform, but, hey, this is Italy!

I was fascinated by the two enormous raised signal cabins that controlled the approaches to Milan Central station. One of the original Class 444 Bo-Bo electrics that the Italian railways officially branded 'Tortoises' arrives at the terminus with a twelve coach inter-city train on 30 April 1994, while on the left a Bo-Bo diesel electric shunting locomotive of the D145 type awaits the 'right away' to drag an empty sleeping car train to the sidings. Pity about the electrification pole that clips the view of the front of the diesel, but at least it strengthens the framing of the express train in the picture. The Class 444 electrics were subsequently life extended, but with a less individualistic appearance.

On a visit in 1995 to the preservation centre at the former Carnforth depot in Lancashire, I was pleased to see the Southern Railway's 1926-built 4-6-0 850 *Lord Nelson* standing inside the shed near the southern doorway. This locomotive is part of the National Collection. While working in the north of England, this locomotive performed well on duties over the Settle & Carlisle line. It is likely that its long firebox, which some Southern firemen had difficulty in managing, was similar enough to a 'Royal Scot' firebox not to bother London Midland Region crews. Contrasty lighting like this can mute any colours in the picture, as it has partially done here, so the image could just as easily be rendered in black-and-white. I used Photoshop to attempt to darken the brightest areas, otherwise they would have appeared completely bleached out.

In 1992, Her Majesty the Queen formally opened the Dargan bridges in Belfast. These carry the start of the M2 and M3 motorways as well as the single track of what was then a new railway link. The railway connects the north end of Belfast Central station with the northbound route out of the former terminus at Belfast York Road that served Larne and Londonderry. Belfast Central is itself a relatively modern through station that was opened in 1976 and had enabled Great Victoria Street and Queen's Quay termini to be closed. After the bridge was opened, York Road station was replaced by a small through station nearby, and the terminus was converted for use as a depot. Happily, a new station on the Great Victoria Street site was opened in the 1980s as an adjunct to the main bus station, closer to the centre of Belfast than Central railway station is! This photograph shows a Class 80 diesel electric multiple unit of Northern Ireland Railways crossing the River Lagan on its way towards Derry.

The former Great Northern Railway (Ireland) station at Dublin Amiens Street, now renamed Connolly, sports this fine Italianate façade to the main building. The station is in two parts, the original GNR(I) terminus which is still complete and busier than ever, and the three through platforms on viaducts just off to the left of the picture, that continue to serve DART (Dublin Area Rapid Transit) and outer suburban trains to the north and south of Dublin as well as main line trains to Rosslare. Just opposite the main station building is the North Star Hotel which had its reception desk sited underneath one of the DART line bridge arches!

My wife and I came across this scene quite by accident. In May 1995, we were travelling by train across Germany, heading towards Dresden, when at Halle we espied members of the public walking around a siding with some classic old electric locomotives clearly on display. We were intrigued enough to bail out of the train and make our way to what turned out to be a depot having a locomotive festival. After enjoying the old electrics and also photographing a 'Flying Hamburger' diesel set, I ventured over a footbridge, and this is the unexpected scene I saw! Grouped round a turntable in a half-roundhouse was a selection of many of the finest steam locomotives that formerly ran on the German railways. On the turntable is an East German Class 01 rebuild, now Class 01⁵; behind it to the left is 01.150; then 01.137; light pacific 03.001; 03.1010 (a DR rebuild); 23.105, the last steam locomotive built for Deutsche Bundesbahn in 1960; 44.1486, a three-cylinder heavy freight 2-10-0; 52.8154, a DR update of the standard DR war 2-10-0; and 03.204. There was also a classic Saxon 2-6-0 in the line-up, just outside the range of the camera. Wow!

In 1995 PKP (Polskie Koleje Państwowe) ran their second celebration of 150 years of railways in Poland. 1992 had covered 150 years of the railways in the west of Poland, which had once been part of Germany; the 1995 events covered the 150th anniversary of the first railway that opened actually in the Poland of the time. This was enacted in the capital, Warsaw, in the presence of President Wałęsa himself and many invited guests including the Chairman of the British Railways Board, John Welsby. A cavalcade of old locomotives and railcars arrived and backed out again at the Głowny station, the steam locomotives being driven with their brakes on to make the most smoke and noise! This one is light 4-6-2 Pm36-2. This engine has been a popular performer from the heritage depot at Wolsztyn, from where the British company Wolsztyn Experience operated steam locomotive driving courses.

A block load of Foster Yeoman four-wheeled stone hoppers from Acton yard approaches Wandsworth Road station on 26 April 1996 as an eight-car EMU formation overtakes it on the main line from London Victoria. The freight locomotive is Class 60 Co-Co diesel electric 60040. The four chimneys of the redundant Battersea power station dominate the background. This is a changing scene. A large lime green shelter, an eyesore for current railway photographers, was built for the big scrap merchant on the right of this picture not long after this photograph was taken, and intensive developments are now happening around the power station. It is not just the encroaches of nature's growing trees that ruin favourite photo spots.

I photographed this scene from a new road bridge that had been built to access Pride Park, a new commercial park that was being developed on the site of the closed Derby Locomotive Works. Locomotive 60089 *Brecon Beacons* was passing northbound through Derby station with a rake of empty bogie steel-carrying wagons on 10 September 1997. The locomotive carried the striking colours of LoadHaul, one of the three freight operating companies that British Rail had created to facilitate the sale of its freight business during the privatisation programme. In the event, all three units ended up by being sold as one company, English Welsh & Scottish Railway (EWS). The leylandii trees in the lower left of this photograph are now beginning to encroach on this view, though the nearest ones have been cut down.

The low sun strikes a pattern across the platform at Swanage station as staff prepare the evening dining service, the 'Wessex Belle', on the popular Swanage Railway heritage line in Dorset. The locomotive, BR 2-6-4T 80104, is hidden by the drifting steam and the platform awning supports. Old station trolleys and furniture emphasise the atmosphere of the former days of steam at this Dorset resort. Using Photoshop, I have converted what was a colour image into black-and-white for maximum effect.

Privatisation of the many train operating companies from 1996 brought forth a rash of new train liveries, some of which were quite original for the time. The Midland Main Line company employed First Impressions to deck their HSTs in completely new colours based on 'teal green', even though most bystanders had expected something in maroon in view of the line's Midland Railway heritage. Looking quite impressive, the 09:30 London St Pancras to Sheffield train leaves Leicester on 17 September 1997. It is nice to know that these iconic trains still survive on this route in 2017.

For my sixtieth birthday, Mary treated me to a Jules Verne holiday in southern Africa, which began at Cape Town station. The impressively large Class 25NC 4-8-4 locomotive at the front belies the fact that the railway is narrow gauge, at 3ft 6in between the rails. Because several members of the tour party went forward to see this engine at the start of the trip, the train manager organised some run-pasts on later days in the tour. This class was a development of the famous Class 25 condensing locomotives. These had very long tenders which were able to accept the exhaust steam in total so as to condense it in a network of pipes and radiators. The 25s were able to haul long freight trains across the desert between Kimberley and De Aar, where water was scarce. Some of the 25s were later rebuilt as 25NC and other 25NCs were built new. Many South African Railways locomotives were given names by their crews, usually of ladies known by them such as *Caroline* in this picture. One however was called *Amin*; the driver said it was because it was big, black and covered with badges! This photograph was one of the very last that the author took using black-and-white film.

ABOVE: Having persuaded the tour passengers to step down from the 'Union Limited' train and stand on the bluff overlooking Tunnel 5 on the railway climb to the Montague Pass, the train manager had the train set back to beyond the tunnel, and then pull forward at full throttle for a photographic run-past. This was the dramatic scene as Class 19D 4-8-2 2753 and GMAM Garratt 4-8-2+2-8-4 4122 *Jeni* burst out from the tunnel climbing uphill with their fifteen-coach load. The sound was deafening. The date is 24 February 1998.

RIGHT: Next morning I got up early from my 'Union Limited' sleeping car berth while the train was still stabled at Oudsthoorn and took several photographs in the sunrise light. I had had the weird idea that I could take a picture of the sunrise over the dome of a Garratt, perhaps following the artistic suggestion by C. Hamilton Ellis many decades before when he sketched the sun rising over the dome of St Paul's, in his case the 'Schools' class engine called *St. Paul's*. This is the best result from my short pre-breakfast expedition, looking along the main line to Port Elizabeth with signals and a water tower silhouetted against the early morning sky. The sky colours are repeated in the rails and give the picture a sense of homogeneity. The Garratt was parked in a siding with trees blocking the sun.

Occasionally plans go awry. My friend Alan Thorpe and I decided to have a day on the East Lancashire Railway on 3 October 1998. When we got there, we saw a big crowd of families filling the train standing in Bury Bolton Street station, and all the train engines had silly faces tied to their smokebox fronts. It was Thomas day. Conventional railway photography was out. After retiring hurt for a pub lunch, we ventured forth to Summerseat where the viaduct was a known visual feature, and took photographs from side-on angles that did not show the face on each locomotive. This is Hughes 'Crab' 2-6-0 42765 heading from Bury to Rawtenstall later that afternoon. The colours were so dull that day, that I have made the image monochrome to brighten it up a little!

On 12 June 1999, the Bournemouth Railway Club was given the opportunity to travel on the Moors Valley Railway near Ringwood, Dorset, for an exclusive, out-of-hours evening, subject to making an appropriate donation. This 7¼ inch gauge railway runs by a public park, is fully signalled using track circuits and radios, and has a convoluted route that gives the little engines freedom to run fast and hard despite the many curves. It is a great way of enjoying steam trains in a safe way! Most of the locomotives are home-built at the railway's workshops. In this picture, the line's weed-spraying train is arriving back at base behind a 2-4-0 while a passenger train leaves with a 4-6-0 in charge.

Two Great North Eastern Railway IC225 trains pass at the north end of Newcastle station, as seen from the city's well-known castle. Even though the track layout was very much simplified by BR, and some platforms and sidings were razed for a car park, it is still an interesting scene, particularly when two or more train movements are in view.

This is the classic view of the Landwasser viaduct on the Albula Line, part of the metre gauge Rhätische Bahn in Switzerland. One of the hourly expresses crosses the viaduct in February 1998 behind a modern Ge4/4III Bo-Bo electric locomotive, still in its RhB red livery before any advertising vinyls covered the red. The wagon at the rear carries the car of a driver who did not wish to drive over the snowy pass. This viewpoint temporarily gave me a dose of vertigo.

I then photographed the Landwasser viaduct from further up the valley and was delighted when one of the Ge4/4ᴵᴵ Bo-Bos came across with a short freight train.

Alan Thorpe and I visited Poland in May 1999 and our friend Andrzej from Warsaw enjoyed driving us around to photograph this special steam train that had been chartered by a German group. The locomotive was a former Prussian P.8 4-6-0, owned by PKP, that was by then preserved as part of the national collection and allocated to the museum steam depot at Wolsztyn. Coupled to three 'thunderbox' four-wheeled carriages, Ok1-359 crosses an embankment near Chrypsko on its way from Wolsztyn to Zbąsinek. The locomotive is not quite on the 'third' in the picture because I did not want it to clash with the small telegraph pole; the foreground lane helps to lead the eye to the engine and the lane and loco are both well-framed by the trees.

Cab fronts face each other at Ipswich, as the sidings alongside the station host several stabled electric and diesel locomotives in BR's corporate freight livery. Nearest the camera are two Class 86s, then with Freightliner embellishments added; they are coupled for multiple working of a heavy container train from Felixstowe that they will take over at Ipswich and drag round the North London Line to head north on the West Coast Main Line. Behind them is a Class 47 or 56, also in freight livery. Because the Felixstowe branch is not electrified, diesel locomotives are needed for the initial short haul.

During the period when I was commissioned to put together some books on locomotive liveries, I took this study of the side of Bo-Bo electric 90023 at Crewe station on 7 September 1999. The locomotive is neatly branded 'Railfreight Distribution' in BR's corporate rail alphabet style. The livery involves three different shades of the colour grey, a potentially dull colour that actually looked very smart when locomotives were kept clean, as was this one.

CHAPTER 7

THE 2000S – MODERN TRAINS AND WORKING STEAM THE WORLD OVER

The first decade of the twenty-first century was notable for several reasons. It marked a considerable expansion of my travels, to more and farther-distant countries. It marked the onset of the digital revolution in popular photography. In the UK, the twenty-first century saw our privatised railways expand their passenger traffic beyond anyone's dreams, to the point that overcrowding returned in many areas forcing railway managers and politicians to engage in seeking ways of increasing the capacity of the railway network, not always succeeding.

The early years of the decade introduced me to the delights of travel in China, India and Myanmar. People have asked how Mary and I kept well during our Indian journeys knowing that many tourists have suffered with a condition known as 'Delhi belly'. One of my former BR colleagues, Dr David Boocock (no proven relation), had once spent five weeks in India and he told me that he and his wife had always cleaned their teeth in whisky before going to bed; this would tackle any stray bacteria in their mouths and beyond, he said. Also, Mary and I noticed early on how strong and wiry many Hindus were despite their vegetarian diet, so Mary and I tried that, too; we avoided meat for the whole time we were in India. The combination of the two methods worked for us!

In 2004, I was also able to realise one of my more outlandish dreams. On many of our longer train journeys across Europe we had previously enjoyed the outward travel, which often lasted two or three days, but sometimes became a bit bored having to retrace our steps to get back home. Supposing instead we continued three more days and the same again, *ad infinitum*, we could actually travel round the world by train given a long enough time! That idea grew until I decided I thought I had a really good excuse – September 2004 marked my having worked for the railways in one capacity or another for fifty years, and that needed celebrating. But I felt that if we were to indulge ourselves with such a long and expensive holiday, someone else ought to benefit from it. So we used our already-established links with the UK charity Railway Children, and agreed a way to use our trip to support the charity by raising funds and increasing awareness of it in other countries. We also had to beat Phileas Fogg and his journey of 80 days around the world!

This coincided with my acquisition of a digital single lens 'reflex' (DSLR) camera, a Konica-Minolta A1. After all, I had had photographs published from my first digital camera which was a two-megapixel compact that had been part of a bundle when I bought a new computer in 2002. I was soon able to get good results from my new DSLR camera, its main disadvantage in my experience being the accessibility of its many operating buttons which were in places around the body where it was humanly only too easy to press a button when one did not intend to. At the time, five million pixels seemed enough for publishable pictures.

Our round-the-world route took us across Europe and Russia, through Mongolia and into China and thence across South-East Asia to Singapore, almost all by train. A Qantas flight to Perth put us on the 'Indian Pacific' train to reach Sydney. We had a quick look at New Zealand, and then spent a few weeks in South America, the highlight of our tour in many ways. Going north through the Americas to Halifax, Nova Scotia, took us to the geographic limit of inter-city rail in Canada. We crossed Ireland by train and re-entered England via through Holyhead and North Wales. We finished within seventy-six days. And we had visited both hemispheres, which Phileas Fogg had not; in our view, he cheated by not crossing the Equator, and we had beaten his record by four days!

Digital memory cards in 2004 were nothing like as capacious as they are today. During our long trip, we adopted a policy of finding IT/photo shops where the pictures we had taken could be printed and also put on CD, two in fact. We posted one CD home with the prints and travelled with the second CD. This enabled the images on the memory cards to be deleted and the cards re-used. We did this approximately every three weeks, in Singapore; Sydney; Bariloche, Argentina; and in New Orleans. We did not repeat that in Canada, which was a pity because my camera bag was stolen from under our feet in a food hall in underground Montreal and I lost all my USA and Canadian photographs from the trip, and my passport, which is a different story. Luckily, Mary had enough pictures in her camera, so my plan to create a digital slide show of the tour would not have an obvious gap in coverage.

Another difficulty resulting from the limiting capacity of memory cards led me to delete some of the less important pictures in my camera to make room for more photographs on the cards. My camera did not like this and corrupted two cards during the deleting process, one in Australia and one in Argentina. I fully intended to bring these cards home and find software that could read those pictures that were corrupted, but these memory cards were also in the stolen camera case, so my 'plan B' was frustrated. Thankfully, no other digital camera has done this to me since then, and I have never heard of anyone else being so afflicted.

The loss of my passport led us to the British Consul in Montreal who was exceptionally helpful. Within three hours, he had furnished me with an emergency passport valid for the rest of our trip. Now that that consulate is closed, I wonder how travellers with such problems get on. Our tickets for the evening's overnight train to Halifax were also gone with the stolen bag, but the booking office staff at Montreal Central station replaced them without demur for a small fee.

My replacement camera – thank goodness for insurance companies! – was the next version, the Konica-Minolta A2 with eight million pixels, which served me well until 2008. During my fourth railway tour of China, the rain was so persistent that the camera became wet more than once. I discovered the hard way that digital cameras with their electronic controls cannot cope with rain. After one false dawn when it performed well for a day after drying out the first time, the next soaking it got caused it to give up completely. It was a year before I was able to coax any further life out of that camera. Thankfully my lovely wife had allowed me to bring her Canon Powershot 80 digital compact camera with me on that trip, and it performed superbly well as my back-up, producing some eminently-publishable photographs that have appeared in print.

So, a replacement for the rained-off Konica A2 was becoming essential. By that time Konica, who had taken over Minolta in the late 1990s, had itself been taken over by Sony. Sony had developed a range of cameras which I believe took full advantage of Minolta's excellent optics and combined them with Sony's advanced photo-image processing expertise. My new Sony Alpha 200 DSLR was an excellent purchase, having superb optics and a ten million pixels processor: the manager in our local Jessops store insisted that Sony would soon overtake Canon and Nikon in sales of quality cameras. While that has not happened yet, I am sure that Sony cameras are among the best for producing quality images. I bought a rain-proof bag with a lens window for operating the camera in wet weather while keeping it dry, and used it to good effect during a week of incessant rain in Japan in summer 2009. The Alpha 200 is still my main camera for railway photography as I write this chapter.

One huge advantage is that this camera has a range of 'film speeds' from ISO 100 to 3,200. The higher the number, the faster the image sensor. I use ISO100 as standard because that gives me the best image quality in terms of resolution and noise ('grain'). Inside buildings, or on very dull days, I find ISO400 enables me to produce up to A4 pictures without significant deterioration. From ISO800 upwards there is increasing noise, starting in the shadow areas and at the highest speeds covering the whole picture so that resolution is fuzzy when enlarged a lot. There are more modern cameras around now that have bigger receptors that will therefore produce even sharper images, higher resolution and far less noise at very fast speeds. Maybe I shall buy one, one day.

Despite the initial learning curves, I have persevered with digital photography since early 2004 and have never used a film since then. I feel very positive about the change. The ability to see the results straight away on the small camera screen, and to retake photographs at the time if the opportunity is there, is valuable. The image quality I am now attaining is either as good as or better than anything I had achieved with film. I am delighted by the much higher capacity of modern memory cards, and by the performance of my 2005-purchased Canon digital projector. Our round-the-world trip spawned my subsequent touring of clubs and societies with digital slide shows through which Mary and I have been able to collect nearly £30,000 for the Railway Children charity.

I now send only digital images to publishers – this is how they prefer to receive them in any case. Even images from slides or old negatives are better dealt with by scanning them and getting the best out of them using software such as Adobe Photoshop Elements; so much cheaper than the full-blown professional Photoshop. All the pictures in this book have been either scanned, if on film, or they are originally digital. All have been put through Photoshop Elements to get their tones suitable for publication. Apart from removal of the worst instances of projecting telegraph poles and correcting verticals, they have not otherwise been doctored, unless I have said so in the captions, and those photographs are in a distinct minority.

In Appendix 2, I discuss some of the techniques that have evolved during my years with digital photography, particularly in relation to the somewhat peculiar needs of railway photography.

The photographs in this chapter include more of steam trains and overseas railways than one might have expected for the first decade of the twenty-first century. This is because my travels sought out some of the remaining pockets of steam operation in accessible parts of the world while they still existed, mainly in industrial locations. I am not one for chasing steam specials around the UK railways, fun though they are for many people. I prefer to remember steam locomotives working for their living, including working on some of the delightful heritage railways that have sprung up in recent decades.

China was a magnet for railway enthusiasts in the 1990s and 2000s because it still used large steam locomotives in significant numbers on industrial railways, many of them hauling prodigious loads. China is also attractive now because of the

very fast and interesting modernisation of its main line railways, including building from scratch in just fifteen years the world's largest network of high speed railways. These are not yet the common transport mode that very high speed trains have become in Japan, France and Spain, but they soon will be.

So, my railway photography in the 2000s has covered a mixed range of subjects. In this chapter, the emphasis on overseas railways, visited because of the lure of steam, is partially balanced by scenes from the more modern railways of the world.

Minolta X-300 35mm SLR

The year 2000 saw Mary and me travelling extensively on the European continent as well as in the UK. We joined the Railway Touring Company's (RTC) two-weeks tour of Ukraine tantalisingly called 'Steam and snow in the Carpathians' and travelled around that country in the luxury Dzerelo train that was made up of comfortable Soviet-style sleeping cars that must once have been reserved for senior party members or politicians. We also had a splendid restaurant car and a bar/lounge car, in which some of the crew expertly performed traditional Ukrainian songs during dark evenings. Being based on Russian railway technology, the heating on the carriages was by coal stoves; each coach had a stove at the end of the vehicle, warming water that was fed through radiators in the compartments. Effective, but labour-intensive. Each car had its own attendant who did the cleaning, coaling, keeping the coke samovar going for constant hot water for drinking and for enlivening pre-packed pot-noodles, and attending to any specific needs. There was a pretty nurse on board who offered medical help to anyone not feeling well. All in all, this was a luxury experience in a traditional old train. The picture shows two of the former Soviet Union's biggest steam express engines, Class P36 4-8-4s 050 and 064 during a photographic run-past west of Samy on the line from Zhytomir to Lvov as dusk was approaching on 27 February 2000. The railways in the former Soviet Untion countries use a wider track gauge than elsewhere in Europe, namely 5feet instead of 4feet 8½inches.

On one of the last days of the Carpathian railtour, our train crossed the border into Romania and out again at a point where the railway had been affected by border changes as a result of historic conflicts. The train entered Romania at Valea Vişaului, and went back into Ukraine after calling for Romanian passport and customs exit checks at Sarasau. The railway between these two places is dual-gauge with four interlaced rails. After leaving Sarasau and before reaching the Ukraine border, that is in no-man's land out of sight of officialdom, our leader organised one more run-past! Here Russian-style 0-10-0 freight locomotive Er-799-79 glints in the evening sun about fifteen minutes before crossing back into its home country. This class is one of a group that represents the most numerous class of locomotives ever built anywhere in the world. The Class E 0-10-0s numbered over 10,000 at their peak.

BR managed a particularly excellent restoration job on the two large London, Chatham & Dover Railway crests at the south of Blackfriars railway bridge in London; one is seen on the right of this picture. The bridge crosses the River Thames and today carries local trains to Kent as well as Thameslink trains. On 12 April 2000, a Thameslink Class 319 EMU crosses the bridge with St Paul's cathedral dominating the background. This picture is no longer possible because Blackfriars station has been rebuilt to cover the whole length of the bridge.

ABOVE: When the Stephensons built the railway across North Wales to reach Holyhead they tried to match the splendour of Conwy castle by building castellated ends to the tubular railway bridge, which spanned the Conwy river just south of the original Telford road bridge. With so much heritage at hand, a Northern Rail two-car Class 158 DMU looks quite insignificant as it heads west, away from Llandudno Junction on 20 April 2000.

LEFT: The small seaside resort of Portrush in Northern Ireland has several points of interest, in particular its ancient somersault signals and its often atrocious weather. Both are evident in this shot of a Northern Ireland Railways 'Castle' class diesel electric multiple unit leaving the Portrush terminus on 17 May 2000 on its way to Coleraine where it will connect with trains to Belfast and to Londonderry. The signal is one of the very last somersault semaphore signals to be used in the UK, and was expected to be replaced by modern signals in 2016. For most of the time recently, the signalboxes on this branch line have been switched out while only one train was allowed on the branch at a time. The signalboxes were manned only when there were special workings around, such as the RPSI steam specials. When taking this photograph, Alan Thorpe and I watched the rainstorm cross the headland opposite, then obliterate the view of the harbour, before hitting the town and drenching everything and everybody in its path. Bright sunshine was to follow the storm, with the blue sky already showing in this picture.

I joined the Railway Touring Company's tour of South Africa in August 2000, probably the best-organised steam train tour for railway enthusiasts I had ever been on. The tour used the 'Union Limited' train of pre-war sleeping cars and was hauled by no fewer than twenty-three different steam locomotives of seventeen different classes during the two weeks. One of the most spectacular run-pasts happened on 8 August just before breakfast, when a group of hardy photographers stood with water lapping at our feet to watch the train cross the Knysna causeway bridge with the sunrise behind the train. Two Class 19D 4-8-2s 2749 and 3324 headed the train. This run-past was cleverly staged by the train manager who timed the departure from Knysna exactly right to create these spectacular lighting conditions.

The next day the 'Union Limited' train headed northwards behind Class 24 2-8-4 3693 and 19D 4-8-2 2698. Here it takes the sharp curve at Antonie. In the background is the unusually-formed Swartberg mountain ridge.

A visit to the Straßhof locomotive museum north of Vienna in Austria is always interesting because of the wide range of Austrian locomotives held there for posterity. On 10 June 2001, this enormous 2-8-4 express locomotive was at the back of the engine shed. 12.10 was one of a class of thirteen such giants that were built to pull heavy express trains over the gradients of the Wienerwald on the Austrian Westbahn. In post-war years, at least two of them spent some time on the Semmering line linking the capital over the Alps with Graz and countries beyond. The type was copied for Romanian railways which had numerous difficult main lines, and seventy-nine were built in that country. A preserved example of these has been sold to Austria, restored to working order, and now masquerades as ÖBB 12.14. The Straßhof depot museum exudes the atmosphere of a genuine working depot when there are special trains around, say, at a celebration or festival.

My first visit to China was on a week-long trip in 2001 organised by Bill Alborough and advertised as his 'China cheapie'. It served to show me the potential of China as an expanding country and to appreciate the railways there and to get to know something of these interesting and friendly people. Steam traction continued on a number of industrial railways long after it had been dismissed from the national railways. The railway in Inner Mongolia that ran northwards from the mines at Daliuta to the steelworks at Baotou was opened in 1996. New diesels were not at first available so a fleet of about twenty-five large Class QJ 2-10-2 steam locomotives was brought in for the job of moving coal from the mines to the steelworks over about 100miles distance. Part of the route was uphill, and to lift trains of forty-eight loaded bogie coal wagons necessitated thee of these powerful machines, two at the front and one pushing from the rear. Such a train is seen in this view of the approach to AoBaoGou on 30 October 2001. Later, we saw that two new Class DF4 Co-Co diesel-electrics could do the work of three of these steam locomotives on this line.

Not far from the summit at Ghum on the Darjeeling Himalayan Railway in India is the Batasia Loop. The idea of loops is to enable railways to gain height by following a circular path while climbing and then crossing over the same track on a bridge. In this picture, which shows a downhill train on the outer edge of the upper part of the loop, the bridge is just in front of the house, the red roof of which is visible near the bottom left. After passing under the bridge, the downhill train will continue paralleling the upper track at the lower level until it makes its way down the side of the Hill Cart Road on the right of this view. The monument in the centre of the loop commemorates the Gurkha Regiment's achievements and sacrifices; this is after all a Gurkha district. The 'Last Post' is played at sunset. On a clear day, Mount Kanchenjunga is visible in the background, though on 30 January 2002 it was hidden by a blue haze.

A visit to India and Myanmar, the beautiful country previously called Burma, was run by Enthusiast Holidays in early 2002. The tour included a couple of days on the enigmatic Burma Mines Railway that serves an aluminium smelter at Namtu in the north of the country. The railway was giving free rides to residents in the valley using road lorries converted to run on the narrow gauge tracks. The tour group chartered one of the railway's museum locomotives, Bagnall 0-4-2T No. 13, for a run uphill to the mining village at the end of the line. The train crew chose this delightful spot to pause for their mid-morning break.

In the north-east of England the Beamish Outdoor Museum displays Victorian streets, working trams, trolleybuses, mining equipment and trains from bygone ages. One track is used for live steam runs hauled by modern working replicas of pioneering locomotives from the early nineteenth century. This one, seen on 29 March 2002, is *Elephant*, a 0-6-0 colliery engine modelled on one dating from 1815 with a train of splendid imitations of early railway carriages. Other locomotives there include a replica of George Stephenson's *Locomotion No. 1* from the 1925 opening of the Stockton & Darlington Railway, and a strangely-laid-out representation of Trevethick's Pen-y-Daren tramway engine of 1804.

Seen from a hilltop overlooking Durham's fine railway viaduct on 8 April 2002, a southbound Great North Eastern Railway IC225 train leaves Durham station on a working from Edinburgh to London King's Cross. These push-pull trains are worked by Class 91 Bo-Bo electric locomotives under 25kV catenary. The carriage sets are former British Rail mark 4 vehicles, designed like the locomotives for operation up to 140mph, hence the appellation 'InterCity 225' where 225km/h equals 140mph, a speed still unattainable on the East Coast Main Line until the signalling is upgraded from 125mph, if that ever happens. Most of these trains will soon be displaced by Hitachi Class 800 series trains.

The Railway Touring Company runs trips to the Italian Mediterranean island of Sardinia most years, using the 950mm gauge minor railways there for touring that pleasant land. On 28 May 2002, 2-6-0T No. 5 worked a charter train from Bosa on the west coast of the island. The climb inland from the seaside town afforded superb views such as this one with the ancient citadel guarding the harbour entrance in the background. This engine proved to be a bit feeble, and lost quite a lot of time during the morning. I have seen no reports of its use on tour trains in later years.

My second trip to China included a visit to the steelworks at Anshan, east of Beijing and not so far from the North Korean border. This particular day dawned dark and polluted. The light on our arrival at the works was very low, such that on 400ASA film I could only use an exposure of 1/30 at f/3.5 after 11am. It then became very much darker (!), with the proposed shutter speed down to 1/5th second. We all retired to the bus, and stayed there until a heavy rain storm had almost passed by. Only two of us ventured out for a quick look after the storm, this picture being one result. It shows Class SY 2-8-2 No. 1035 resting while hot ladle wagons are loaded with molten steel under the blast furnaces. Some people deplore the sight of heavy industry as a blot on the landscape, but I like a suitable industrial background to a picture where it is appropriate and suitably dramatic like this one certainly is.

I had met a friend in London on 9 July 2003 during the break while his tour train got ready for its return journey from Waterloo to Weymouth. I then took a local train to Vauxhall to photograph the train as it headed back to the south-west, and this was the lucky result. Ex-BR Class 5 4-6-0 73096 put out sufficient smoke to blur the ugly background office blocks, and most unusually there were no other trains in the picture on this busy railway. This locomotive is liveried in BR lined green, and the train it was hauling was made up of coaches owned by the Mid-Hants Railway with authorisation at that time to run on Railtrack tracks. The set-up was always known colloquially as 'the Green Train'.

Konica-Minolta A1 digital 'SLR'

ABOVE: In the early days of digital cameras, it was a well-known adverse feature of many that, when you pressed the button, the camera delayed taking the photograph by a second or more; this would be useless for photographing fast-moving trains. So, soon after buying my first digital SLR, I wanted to see how well it performed in this respect. This led me to visit Tamworth station, where the low level platforms flank the Up and Down fast lines of the West Coast Main Line. By early 2004, the new Virgin Pendolino units were in full command of the fast trains. I discovered immediately that my new camera was excellent; when I pressed the shutter release button it instantaneously took the picture. This image was the result of photographing a Class 390 passing through Tamworth at about 80mph, with the shutter priority set at 1/1000th second.

RIGHT: As two Eurostar trains on the London run await departure from Paris Gare du Nord on 10 April 2003, a TGV arrives from the Lille direction. The success of high speed rail in Europe is challenging air as the preferred means of travel between major cities, as in Japan. My wife always chides me for disappearing out of a train to take photographs after we have boarded, shouting 'Make sure you get back on!'

On a trip to Switzerland in March 2004, this was the scene at Ospizio Bernina after the winter snows had been repeatedly ploughed and the platforms cleared of snow over and over again. The Rhätische Bahn runs hourly services over all its tracks, more in some areas, despite the weather. All its trains carry low-level snowploughs, and track maintenance machines with wider ploughs patrol the tracks regularly when snow is falling. The 'Bernina Express' is one of the favourite tourist trains in the area and is equipped with modern 'panoramic' carriages. I was shouted at by the guard as I took this photograph, and I had to leap back into the coach so as not to delay this important train.

Old survivors invite photography! One of the earliest 25kV electric locomotives in Europe that were built from the 1950s, first for France and then a few for Luxembourg, arrives at Bettembourg in the latter country on 1 April 2004 with the 16.45 from Athus to Luxembourg city. This was just two years before the whole class was rendered obsolete by more modern locomotives and a fleet of new multiple units, and well after such characterful machines had ceased working passenger trains in France. I do not regard the many verticals on the platform as a distraction in this picture as they act to hide the rear of the train and push the eye towards the strange-looking locomotive. Neither is the overhead wiring in the sky a distraction; it is surely part of the scene on any electrified railway that uses overhead wires. The fairly contrasty lighting of the train is enough to keep the viewer's attention.

In July 2004 I took Mary to Slovenia and we enjoyed a lovely day out from Goriza on the daily summer steam train to Lake Bled, a wonderful setting of a lake amidst Alpine mountains. On the day of our trip, the engine was former Yugoslav Railways 2-10-0 33-037. This is one of the many German war-time austerity freight engines that found their way into other countries during and after the Second World War. Germany built about 7,000 of these useful machines as part of its war effort.

The craziest thing Mary and I ever did together was to go round the world by train, which we did in 2004. In New Zealand, I was granted a footplate permit for the electrified main line between Hamilton and Palmerston North, a single track route through the mountains on North Island. At a passing loop our daily passenger train, the 'Overlander', had to wait for this container train to pass. The two locomotives were built in the UK by Brush of Loughborough. They are NZR Class EF Bo-Bo-Bos and work on the 25kV system. It was nice to see a rare example of modern UK locomotive exports in active service! As I write this, Kiwi Rail is consulting on de-electrifying this section of railway in favour of keeping the diesel locomotives on the train for the whole distance between Wellington and Auckland.

In Argentina, the country that we regarded as the highlight of our round-the-world tour in 2004, we travelled from Esquel on the Saturdays-only tourist train on the line that the British call 'the Old Patagonian Express' but which the locals call 'La Trochita'. The line runs in the shadow of the Andes and for over one hundred miles crosses the desert of central Patagonia, though the Saturday tourist trains only run for about an hour from each end. Our engine was a Henschel-built 2-8-2, 750mm gauge. The train included a bar. Two groups of singers entertained the passengers. When we arrived at the outer terminus, Nahwel Pan, we saw some locomotives and carriages stored in open sidings there. The desert air is dry, which considerably delays any deterioration. It was pleasing to see that numberplates and builders' plates were all still intact on the stored locomotives; there are clearly no vandals in the area.

Konica-Minolta A2 digital 'SLR'
On 31 March 2005, my friend Alan Thorpe and I visited the iron ore railway that carries heavy ore traffic from the mines at Kiruna in Sweden to the North Sea port of Narvik in Norway. At that time, the older electric locomotives of class Dm3 were gradually being replaced by new locomotives. One of the old-timers, a triple unit locomotive of 1D-D-D1 wheel arrangement, drifts downhill through Abisko Turiststation with a standard rake of fifty-two empty bogie hopper wagons, each of 100tonnes gross weight when loaded. I found these machines fascinating to watch. Their three sets of coupled wheels were thrashing round usually out of phase with each other and gave an impression of power, which their 5,000bhp output potential amply confirmed. The locomotives dated from between the early 1960s to the 1970s. All were finally withdrawn in the 2010s.

ABOVE: On the same day, a pair of brand new Bombardier Co-Co locomotives passes Abisko Turiststation with a loaded train of iron ore weighing all of 5,200tonnes. More recently the railway has been upgraded to an axle load of 30tonnes, the heaviest on a European main line, I believe. These Co-Co+Co-Co pairs now haul trains of new wagons of 120tonnes gross each, the trains being longer and weighing over 8,200tonnes! There are two stations at Abisko, the other being Abisko Östra, and both are good for railway photography, with several different spots in the area for changes of angle. There is a useful tourist centre near the Touriststation that offers accommodation and that has a cafeteria and facilities.

RIGHT: In October 2005, Mary and I revisited the United States and Canada to take some photographs to replace those that disappeared when my camera case was stolen in Montreal the year before. In Chicago on 4 October, we stood for half an hour on top of a multi-storey car park taking pictures of the well-known Loop railway, probably the best surviving North American 'elevated' line. At the famous crossing where two double-track railways cross each other and also interconnect on three corners, an Orange Line train draws a bright arc from the conductor rail as it curves round from the west to the north side of the central loop section. It is hard to realise looking down on the railway that there are two main roads underneath that also cross here!

During a ski holiday in Austria, my wife concluded that three days skiing instruction was enough to bear. She decided instead to join me on my travels around the Alps on trains. So, on 22 February 2006, we found ourselves on the Zillertalbahn's tourist train headed by the line's ex-Yugoslav 0-8-2 83-076. The picture was taken as the train approached the Erlach bridge en route from Jenbach to Mayrhofen.

The year after the Syrian army had at last relinquished its occupation of the Beqa'a Valley in Lebanon, our tour group was able to visit the railway depot and workshops at Rayak. No work had been done there since the railway had been abandoned during fighting that started in 1976, leaving all the locomotives standing where they were when work stopped. This powerful 0-10-0T rack-and-adhesion engine had once been used on part of the hilly railway that linked Damascus with Beirut. On 31 May 2006, it was sitting on the jacks in Rayak works awaiting return of its wheelsets which were under repair. It had sat there for thirty years, the jacks and all its components rusting gently; it may even still be there now! The clutter on the floor is mainly roofing tiles. Bill told us the tiles had been shot down by the departing Syrian army.

I just could not resist joining Bill Alborough's trip to the Hedjaz Railway as it covered this historically important railway from Jordan through Syria and into Lebanon, albeit with only a few short-distance train rides. We were much further north than the section of the railway in Saudi Arabia where Lawrence of Arabia caused so much damage, most of which has not been repaired, but from Aqaba in Jordan to Damascus in 2006 the railway was complete, at least until the subsequent civil war broke out in Syria. On 28 May 2006, the tour group chartered a steam train from Dera'a to travel down the Yarmouk Gorge, nowhere near as far as the railway used to go (Haifa), not even to the Israeli border. But at least it was a very pleasant day, the Syrians treated us well, and organised several run-pasts such as this one over a handsome steel bridge. The locomotive is an oil-fired Hartmann 2-8-0 that was fired up for us at very short notice when the intended Mallet tank developed leaks in the firebox. The track gauge is 1.05metres, an odd gauge chosen to prevent other countries running their military trains on it during hostilities.

We took our eldest two granddaughters and their mother to visit the Birkenau camp at Auschwitz (Oswięcim) on 13 February 2007. After we had walked past the destroyed gas chambers, we reached the end of the railway line that had brought about one and a half million people to their untimely and undeserved deaths. There I saw this wreath that someone had placed between the rails. It bore on a red ribbon the motif, in German, 'Never forget'. I felt that printing the picture as a monochrome with just the wreath in colour would fit the atmosphere of mourning that still pervades that appalling place.

One of my favourite spots in the whole of the British Isles is Downhill, just to the west of Castlerock in Northern Ireland. On a rare and beautiful day when, looking north, one could clearly see the Scottish Isle of Islay across the sea, this spot above the high cliffs can bring a sense of peace and appreciation of nature's beauty. The railway between Belfast and Londonderry runs underneath the Downhill estate in two tunnels and then skirts the fabulous wide beach under the high cliffs before it reaches the right bank of Lough Foyle and then on to the city of Derry. On the railway in this picture, taken on 15 May 2007, is one of Northern Ireland Railways' then-new Spanish-built DMUs, No. 3004. In the distance across the mouth of the lough is a glimpse of the hills of County Donegal in the republic, the most northerly county in the whole of Ireland.

The tour operator that was later to take us to India, Darjeeling Tours, also offered a trip to the Vivarais railway in central France, which Mary and I jumped at. The railway was an icon of French narrow-gauge byway railways, and had some particularly unusual features. It shared about a kilometre stretch of electrified main line railway with the French national operator, SNCF, and had a fleet of steam locomotives that included some Mallet articulated tank engines as well as an assortment of ancient diesel railcars. On 13 July 2007, 0-6-6-0T Mallet No. 414 brings the daily tourist train out of the Chemin de Fer du Vivarais' Tournon station onto the mixed gauge track and approaches a tunnel, beyond which the CFV line branched westward up the valley to Lemâstre where its passengers would enjoy a very long, French lunch. Nowadays track sharing is no more. The Vivarais line starts from its formerly first intermediate station.

On the Darjeeling Himalayan Railway, a team of five railwaymen attempt to release the jammed brakes of the first coach of a charter train at Tindharia station on 12 March 2008, while others look on. This railway is part of the Indian Hill Railways World Heritage Site, and climbs for 55 miles to a height of around 7,000feet at its summit at Ghum. Its steam locomotives include some built in the 1880s. This is 786 *Ajax*. Any incident in India is sure to attract a crowd! The engine's coal bunker is above the firebox, and a man rides on it shovelling coal down a chute to the fireman in the cab. The two standpoints with handrails at the locomotive front are for the sandmen, two guys who dribble sand on the rails by hand if adhesion conditions require it. With the driver, fireman, coalman and two sandmen, this little engine has a crew of five.

The Jalainur opencast coal mine in northern China was for many years the place where one could see more standard gauge steam locomotives working together than anywhere else in the world. The mine was four kilometres long, half a kilometre wide and half a kilometre deep. This view shows, towards the right, the deep hole from which coal was still being extracted on 14 September 2008, its small area indicating that the mine was almost worked out. It has since closed. In this picture are about thirteen trains, all worked by standard gauge SY 2-8-2s belonging to the mining company which owned a fleet about thirty strong. A few are handling coal trains while the majority take trains of overburden, zig-zagging up the terraces to a high level for tipping. At least one locomotive is with a track-shifting crane – the tracks had to be moved closer to the work face from time to time as the coal face was cut back by large draglines that had been supplied by Russia. A few years earlier, in 2002, I had stood at the edge of the park overlooking the mine and counted twenty-six steam locomotives working at once in one view!

Sony Alpha 200 DSLR:
Among the finest British Rail electric multiple units were the Class 442 five-car express units built in the mid-1980s for the Bournemouth line. On 13 July 2003, unit 2409 stands at London Waterloo in sight of what was then known as the 'Millennium Wheel', now dubbed the 'London Eye'. The views from the wheel are well worth the expense of spending an hour in one of the pods. The livery of this train was designed by Ray Stenning's firm Best Impressions for South West Trains and incorporates the basic colours of the owning group Stagecoach, but applied with considerable flair, particularly with the bold sweep of red and orange over the leading car's roof. This was practical because SWT's depots have carriage washing machines with roof brushes. The pattern of the foreground platforms adds to the striking impact of this picture. The curved roof between the train and the big wheel is that of the international platforms that were used by Eurostar for their first decade or so. New buildings are gradually changing this view.

The Japanese are disciplined in their leisure as well as at work. Notice how the tourists off a steam excursion at Motegi on 18 July 2009 have been corralled into a safe and railed-off area to watch the ceremony of 'turning the locomotive'. The driver of the engine, Class C12 2-6-2T 66, had pressed a button to start up the electric turntable, and overhead loudspeakers played loud, tinkly music as the locomotive turned round! The track gauge of railways in Japan is 3ft 6in, except for the Shinkansen (high speed railways) which are standard gauge.

Even Japanese trains run late if the forces of nature get in the way, like 2-6-0 No. 58654 in this picture during a downpour that flooded several tracks. This steam special awaiting departure from Hitoyoshi station on the afternoon of 25 July 2009 had been delayed while railwaymen received reports on whether the line was still safe to use before the return journey. During this ten-day tour of Japanese railways, our party experienced nine late trains for various reasons, including a collision between a car and train on a level crossing, though not all delays were explained to passengers. To avoid getting my camera wet, I took this picture with the camera inside a transparent plastic bag which had an aperture for the lens to poke out. The system worked!

Japanese railways are nowadays best known for their network of high speed lines, or *Shinkansen* (new railway). On 26 July 2009, at Shin Yamaguchi one of the 700 series of modern trains capable of 330km/h flashes through on the centre tracks while passengers wait for a following train that will shortly divert to the platform track. Note the water spraying off the leading pantograph as it wipes rain off the overhead contact wire.

CHAPTER 8

THE 2010S – UK RAILWAYS AT THEIR BUSIEST EVER

In the photographic world, the 2010s surely highlight the rise of the mobile phone camera. Indeed, the advent of smartphones, iPads and 'tablets', all equipped with tiny built-in cameras, has brought cheap and instantaneous photography into the hands of the masses. I have to say that I have been astounded at the quality of photographs produced by the camera in my current smartphone, which is not an expensive one. I can rely on being able to get an acceptable image in almost any light; I do not have to think about exposures, ISO ratings, depth of field or anything technical, other than composition and focus point. In normal light, including indoor artificial light, I can take photographs that can be reliably enlarged to A4 size and are often of publishable quality. The phone's camera has a flash if I need it, and it even has a secondary lens at the front so I can take a photo of myself if I really want to! I very rarely ever use flash. Railway subjects are generally too far away to benefit from the reach of a flashgun, and in any case, it is unacceptable to use flash for moving trains because of the risk of damage to a driver's eyesight.

The convenience of my mobile phone means that I no longer need to take a camera with me on most of my travels around the UK, other than when I might want to intervene during serious railway photography. There are some disadvantages, of course. My mobile phone camera has a fixed field of view and manages its own 'shutter speed'. Thus, it is not suitable for photographing fast moving trains, nor for longer distance views that need a long focal length lens. Zooming in on a mobile phone camera is done digitally, which quickly reduces the image quality. Thus, I need my DSLR camera with its two zoom lenses with me on holiday and when taking moving photographs, and for maximum flexibility in composing pictures.

The advent of good mobile phone cameras has coincided with my deep involvement with the Famous Trains model railway charity in Derby. Initially, I brought my camera and tripod into the Famous Trains building when I wanted to take model railway photographs. Then a trustee started running a scratch-built 00-scale model of the LMS 1938 three-car articulated diesel train on a day when I did not have my camera with me. I used my mobile phone camera to photograph the unit – and to announce it on Facebook – and was very surprised at the result, which was better than I could have taken with my camera hand-held. The depth of focus in the image was excellent.

I illustrate in this book the current decade up to the time of writing (2017) with a mixture of pictures taken with my trusty Sony Alfa 200 digital SLR as well as with my successive mobile phones.

The other key feature of the 2010s has been the continued upsurge in passenger numbers on Britain's railways. Bucking previous historical trends, the recession early in the decade did not significantly slow this growth. The result has been an increase in overcrowding on our trains. New trains are on the horizon as I write this, specifically for Northern Rail, the East Coast Main Line and for Great Western, as well as for several London area franchisees, East Anglia, Hull Trains and ScotRail. On the down side, government policy towards 'greener' energy has led to closure of several coal-fired power stations and conversion of others to burn gas or biomass. A result of this has been a substantial fall in rail-borne coal traffic, removing at a stroke many photogenic scenes of coal trains with strings of matching wagons which many modern railway photographers have enjoyed. This trend is likely to continue, bringing the sight of long coal trains in Britain almost to an end within about five years. As is so often the case, this trend started first across the Atlantic; North American railroads have been putting hundreds if not thousands of wagons and locomotives into storage for the same reason for several years.

So, railway photographers will no doubt be making many sorties to take photographs of coal trains in the UK while the opportunity is still there. And they will be chasing after the new passenger trains as they emerge.

We all thought that the 2010s would witness continued progress with electrification of our main lines following completion of the North-Western and Great Western schemes. The major problems being experienced with managing the GWR scheme are already causing delays to other schemes, raising costs amazingly high, and also preventing rolling stock cascades of displaced DMUs to help other areas where there is overcrowding. Photographers who look out for news items will need to keep on their toes to stay up-to-date.

A feature of the modern railway that annoys many photographers is the steady growth of trees and bushes on the lineside over the decades since the end of steam traction. These block views of the railway, views that were previously popular with lineside photographers. Losing useful lineside photographic positions is something photographers have to cope with. It is often a challenge to find somewhere else nearby. Several pictures in this book are now impossible to repeat in a 'then and now' mode. The trees have another down-side: they each shed around 100,000 or more leaves every autumn, and the leaves form a mulch on the rail heads and reduce adhesion to very low levels. Some operators run special timetables to account for the 'defensive driving' that is needed to prevent trains overrunning signals or station platforms during the leaf fall season. This is a bit of a railway 'own goal', really.

After seventy years of taking railway photographs I find myself taking fewer scenes on our UK railways than in previous decades, though I still try to have a record of most types of trains on our network. Instead, I spend more time finding uses for the tens of thousands of photographs in my collection. This book is the twentieth to be published under my name, though that is by no means close to being a record. I write for magazines, and I give several digital slide shows each year to raise funds for that wonderful charity, Railway Children. I still take lots of photographs when on holiday. Mary and I, even at our advancing ages, still prefer to travel across Europe by train if we have the time, and this adds to the opportunities for railway pictures, most of which are scenes that I bump into rather than ones for which I have planned ahead.

I also find that my skills with that excellent tool Adobe Photoshop continue to improve, even though I have been using it for more than a decade now. Its key use for me is to bring out the full tone range of a photograph. It is also useful for resizing pictures which do not need to be vastly huge files if being used as slides in a slide show. Photoshop is good at changing colour pictures into black and white, and for slightly sharpening images. The latest version, I have read, can even compensate for camera shake, but I have not tried that – I'm still on Adobe Photoshop Elements version 9, and the latest as I write this is version 15.

Nonetheless, my attempts at winning photographic competitions, however good I believe my own efforts to be, usually bring me sharply down to earth when I see what others manage to achieve! I have not won anything for several years.

So, what does the future hold for railway photography? This is a difficult question to answer reliably. However, in my opinion, there will always be railways to photograph, at least during the full lifetimes of readers of this book. Current trends suggest that the UK railways will continue to get busier as our main roads and motorways get more and more clogged with traffic. Organised as they are on the lines of many different train operating companies, the current increasing variety of train types and liveries is not likely to diminish, not unless the whole lot gets taken over by a centralised body, which seriously is not likely to happen in my lifetime.

Reopening of more railways is on the cards. Oxford to Cambridge is being talked about now almost as if it is a done deal. I have been lobbying for reopening the Peak Main Line via Bakewell to provide better timings between the East Midlands cities and Manchester, and to provide a faster freight route for aggregate trains from the Derbyshire and West Yorkshire quarries. HS2 will certainly happen, which will clear track space for more, fast regional trains to run on the West and East Coast Main Lines.

All these events will attract railway photographers. Other photographers will continue to visit our many heritage railways, or chase after main line steam specials. In this and the next decade we will see the launching into traffic of a number of brand new steam locomotives. I look forward to seeing the Class P2 2-8-2 2007 *Prince of Wales*, with its alternative name *Duke of Rothsay* when in Scotland, one of Prince Charles's other titles; the 'Saint' 4-6-0 2999 *Lady of Legend*, rebuilt from other mostly standard GWR locomotive parts; the 'Brighton atlantic' 32424 *Beachy Head*; and, if I live long enough, the 'Clan' pacific 72010 *Hengist*. And there are several others that will attract hordes of railway photographers eager to add pictures of them to their own collections including a couple of BR standard tank engines.

Now that it is so easy to share photographs on mobile phones using media such as Facebook and Messenger, I foresee a timely end to wired-in broadband. It cannot be more than five years hence when providers will be able to beam internet access to our computers or other devices like they can to our mobiles and tablets, or like television pictures are beamed to our sets, so telephone lines will surely soon become redundant. Already, some cameras can beam up their photographs to 'the cloud' for storage or for transmission to other people. Telegraph poles beside the railway line, such that exist now, will become an anachronism.

I wonder if we shall eventually see the demise of film photography. A number of photographers doggedly hang on to the use of films, though I am past the point of understanding why they do, apart from the quality of projection. My highest quality photographs have been with three main media: large-format black-and-white negative film; 35mm colour negative film; and modern digital imaging. While other formats such as 35mm black-and-white and colour slides have proved capable of producing adequate A4-size quality prints, only the three first-mentioned media have made it to quality A3-sized printing, at least in my experience. Digital photography improves continually by the inexorable rise in the number of pixels that cameras can produce, and by the continued improvements in image processing by the electronics in cameras, scanners and image processing software.

The capabilities of modern digital photography have already surpassed those I could achieve with film. The future for railway photography looks very bright indeed.

Sony Alpha 200 DSLR camera
The British have always enjoyed being beastly to the French! As a change from dropping off French Eurostar passengers at Waterloo, we now take them to St Pancras station in London where, in 2011, they were confronted with this huge Olympics symbol to remind them that London, not Paris, was to hold the 2012 Olympics. Sir John Betjeman looks somewhat satisfied at the prospect as his statue gazes upwards into Barlow's magnificent overall roof.

Different railways have different standards. Albanian Railways suffer from serious lack of cash, leading to maintainers of locomotives and rolling stock being forced to use second-hand and sometimes inadequate materials. Mary demonstrates here a broken window on a carriage at the capital Tirana's terminus. In the absence of new toughened glass, several windows in this coach had been replaced with thin plate glass like this one; thankfully, this was not typical of the vehicles seen in Albania, even though many at the time had damaged windows; most had been repaired using unbroken windows taken from withdrawn carriages. In this picture, Mary is holding her Canon Powershot digital compact camera. That was well capable of producing some really good quality output, and I used it as my standby camera on my last visit to China; I am glad I did because my own camera failed when it rained too hard on it.

The workers in Shkozet wagon works, Dürres, complained to us foreign visitors that international wagons were arriving in cash-strapped Albania requiring significant repairs before they could be sent back to their owning railways via the rail link to Montenegro. This picture of light-and-shade was taken in that interesting facility in 2010; the van on the right has had its axles withdrawn for bearing repairs.

I got up early on New Year's Day 2011 to photograph the morning air-conditioned express from Bucharest to Braşov passing the village of Poiana Ţupului just north of the ski resort of Sinaia. The train was hauled by one of Romania's splendid life-extended Co-Co electric locomotives, 477-753. This railway route is part of European railway 'corridor IV' that links the Black Sea to the Baltic Sea, which is why Romanian Railways (CFR) are getting EU money to rebuild the railway from the base up to international standards. In this view, the track under the snow to the left of the train has been lifted and the ballast removed in readiness for complete replacement. New overhead electrification structures are also already in place. This work forced CFR to institute single-line working on this main line, which the operators managed with surprisingly reasonable timekeeping.

It must be a mark of a country's high civilisation for a chess board to be available at a capital terminus station for anyone to play! This one was at Budapest Keleti one evening in 2011. The train on the left had arrived in Hungary from Bratislava in Slovakia with a Czech-built electric Bo-Bo at its head. Keleti station is one of Europe's star stations for architectural splendour. It also has a splendid old restaurant that had not been modernised when Mary and I ate there in 2016, and which exudes the atmosphere of former days.

During the 2011 spring gala on the Mid-Hants Railway, the green BR Class 5 73096 arrives at Ropley with a parcels and van train. Note the London & South Western Railway lattice-post signals, the SR-liveried ground frame, and the L&SWR warning notice with just the S and R painted in white, correctly for the Southern Railway period, though my memory of former times suggests that the background should be green. Also note on the right some typical modern lineside clutter left by civil engineers for them to complete a job once the weekend is over! The photographers are all dutifully standing behind the fence.

The very last somersault signals to control train movements on a main line in the United Kingdom were those at Castlerock on the line between Belfast and Londonderry. Until the 2016 resignalling programme, all Down trains used the loop platform; all Up trains used the main platform like Spanish-built (CAF) DMU 3012 that was calling there in May 2014. Since the resignalling, all trains call at the main platform which has been signalled for bi-directional working.

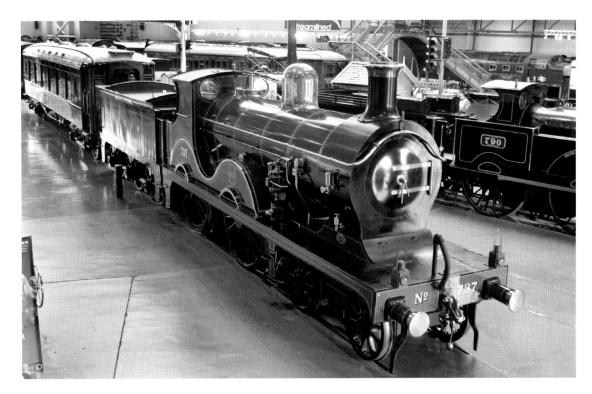

In early 2011, the beautiful South Eastern & Chatham Railway D class 4-4-0 1737 was moved to more visible display in the main hall at the National Railway Museum at York. Designed for working between London and Dover when H. Wainwright was Locomotive Superintendent of the South Eastern Railway, this locomotive carries one of the most ornate colour schemes in the museum. To the right of the picture can be glimpsed London & North Western Railway 2-4-0 790 *Hardwicke*, famous for its active part in the 'railway races to the north' when the L&NW and Caledonian Railways competed with the east coast railway companies to reduce the time taken for trains between London and Aberdeen.

It may look as if this train is running on grass, but the illusion shows how successfully the track of the Oakfield Park Railway is hidden from view from the grand house as it passes across the stately home's lawn! This fifteen-inches gauge line is in a private estate near Raphoe in County Donegal, Ireland, and is open to the public on Saturdays, Sundays and bank holidays and whenever the luscious gardens are open, mainly between April and September. A small diesel locomotive hauls most trains but steam can be available when enthusiast groups book a visit. The steam locomotive is Exmoor-built 0-4-2T *Duchess of Difflin*, and the railway runs a convoluted course of about four kilometres; I found the route's gyrations confused me sufficiently to lose my sense of direction, a rare event indeed!

ABOVE: They would not be allowed to do this in the UK! Spraying water from a hose on the front of a high speed train under 25kV wiring is against current British standards due to the risk of the high voltage electricity arcing back through the spray. One has to assume these railwaymen are aware of the potential danger as they clean the cab front and windows of one of the six-car high-speed trains of Turkish Railways (TCDD) during a stop at Eskişehir between Ankara and Istanbul. During the trip Mary and I took in June 2011, the section to Istanbul was still under construction, so Eskişehir was the temporary terminus of these 250km/h services. I was impressed at the standard of accommodation offered in Turkish main line trains and at the efforts made to keep them all clean.

LEFT: The very short branch line between Stourbridge Junction and Stourbridge in the West Midlands is the stomping-ground of two Parry 'Peoplemovers', small four-wheeled railbuses aimed at low-cost transportation over short distances. One of these is seen in October 2011, climbing towards the Junction station. Somehow the single vehicle that operates the daily schedule manages to cover one out-and-back trip every ten minutes. In this picture, the smallness of the 'Peoplemover' is emphasised by the bulk of the road bridge, which frames the vehicle so that one's eye is drawn to it.

ABOVE: A splendid half day trip for the energetic visitor to the North Yorkshire Moors Railway is to catch a train from one end or other of the line and alight at Newtondale Halt. This single platform has no road access. The only way out is on one of two footpaths. If one takes the left turn, the path eventually leads up the side of Newton Dale, a climb of about five hundred feet to reach the top of the valley that was gouged out by a glacier in the Ice Age. At the time of our visit in July 2012, this Site of Special Scientific Interest (SSSI) was not included in local tourist literature, presumably so as not to disturb its unique flora and fauna. One walk takes the visitor along the top edge of the Dale back towards Levisham and ends at that NYMR station. The depth of the Dale dwarfs S15 4-6-0 825 and its train heading from Pickering to Grosmont.

RIGHT: Later the same day, the S15 stood at Grosmont with a train for Pickering that included, at the front, a former GWR saloon carriage that was booked for a private party. The splendid signal gantry is a strong feature in this picture of 825. I doubt if the young man on the platform got anything like as good a picture with his mobile phone camera from where he is standing! The curve of the platform on the left holds the eye in the picture and the gentle curl of the smoke from 825's chimney neatly embraces the gantry. It is unusual for me to produce square format pictures, but the composition seemed to demand it.

On the occasion of the annual reunion of former engineering apprentices from Eastleigh Locomotive Works in May 2013, Mary and I with some friends enjoyed Pullman car dining on the NYMR. This time the locomotive was one of two Stanier Class 5s in use on the railway that day, 44871. Strong back lighting emphasises the steam blowing off from the engine's safety valves and cylinder drain cocks. This picture would be better with some human interest in it, but it was not to be.

ABOVE: September 2012 saw us take two Turkish-Romanian friends for a holiday in Northumberland, which included a visit to Berwick-upon-Tweed. It was a beautiful day, and a walk alongside the River Tweed enabled me to take several photographs of Robert Stephenson's superb Royal Border Bridge. This one shows an IC225 train crossing the viaduct on an Edinburgh to London King's Cross service. It was sheer good luck how the curve of the clouds in the sky complemented the curve of the train on the bridge. How the original railway got permission to lay its route straight through the site of Berwick Castle, the mind boggles. It could not happen today, could it?

RIGHT: It was a much wetter day when we took our friends on a day out in Edinburgh. After visiting the Royal Mile, the castle and Princes Street we took a DMU to North Queensferry to get a close look at the Forth Bridge. I had not previously seen a picture that brings into focus the bridge and this quayside anchor display. To get this depth of focus I had to stop the lens down to f/10 at 1/160th second, with the camera hand-held and set at ISO200. The depth of focus at a stop of f/10 on a standard digital camera is perhaps equivalent to f/20 on a 35mm film camera with a 50mm lens.

We only had a holiday in north Norfolk in winter once – never again. The stories of the wind off the North Sea blowing straight through you are true! When we visited Weybourne station on the North Norfolk Railway during its Santa specials week, I espied this warm and welcoming fire glowing in the porters' room. This scene could be straight out of the 1940s! In fact, a comment by a friend who liked this picture showed that that young person did not know what a coal scuttle was!

Mary and I were shivering on Weybourne station platform when the signalman beckoned us into his cabin. Inside the signalbox, which is located on the platform opposite the main one, it was warm, and a cup of tea made us feel human again. In preservation, many of the levers are spare, painted white, since the NNR does not need them all for its leaner track layout. The open line telephone is on the right wall at the back of the cabin. Single line tablets are locked in the box near the middle of the photograph, where one can see a hoop used to hold a tablet to make it possible for the signalman and engineman to exchange tablets as the train passes. As trains were just running between Sheringham and Weybourne, the hoop must be for the Holt section tablet.

As part of the promotion for the Famous Trains model railway project in Derby, of which I was chairman until 2016, members of the charity built this small 00-scale branch terminus called Darley Green to take to exhibitions in 2012. The station and yard areas look more realistic than many models because they have been given plenty of space and are not crowded together. The foreground track that leads off to the left was designed to connect with a factory model, shown in the next photograph. The model locomotive is a Hornby Railroad version of the Midland compound 4-4-0 1000, painted in the Midland Railway livery that the original locomotive carried from 1960 when it worked special trains on BR. This scene was photographed with my Sony Alpha 200 standing on a tripod. A nice thing about digital photography is that details of exposure and so forth are recorded in a file attached to the image file, so one can write that the exposure on this occasion was 1/60th at f/22 with speed at ISO800. In the absence of a backscene – since installed – I have filled in the background to hide the clutter that was originally there. Using Photoshop Elements 9, I traced round the outline with the 'Lasso' tool, and filled in the upper area in black.

Members of the Famous Trains model railway charity also built this small 00-scale factory model to take to exhibitions in 2013. The track and points in the factory yard are Hornby Set-track to obtain the necessary sharp-radius curves to fit a small industrial site. Since this photograph was taken, trustee Peter Swift has replaced the plastic point crossings – 'frogs' in modelling terminology – with steel ones to give the short-wheelbase shunting engines a better chance of moving around the yard without losing electrical contact. Most of the buildings are standard Metcalfe card kits. The model now has a realistic backscene attached and is an integral part of the very large model railway that dominates the inside of the Famous Trains building. Photographing this scene necessitated a tripod and the Sony DSLR camera set at 1/60th at f/22 with speed at ISO800. Photoshop Elements came into its own to correct the absurdly leaning verticals caused by the camera angle looking downwards so sharply.

The magazine *Railway Modeller* agreed to run an article on how I modified this Hornby Railroad model with improved livery and detail to represent compound 1000 as it ran in the early 1960s in its pseudo Midland Railway livery. The magazine needed illustrations that had a white background and foreground. To achieve this, I placed the model on some sheets of A3 plain white paper laid on the dining table, with the paper gently curved up behind the model. With the light from the window to one side behind me, I mounted my Sony DSLR on a tripod with the camera set at ISO100 for a fine grain, high resolution image, and the camera set for 'aperture priority', giving an exposure of 1.6 seconds at f/25. The result needed very little tweaking in Photoshop, mainly the whitening of slight shadows on the paper. The resulting image exceeded my wildest expectations.

ABOVE: The nearest heritage railway to our home in Derby is the Ecclesbourne Valley Light Railway (EVLR) which runs from Duffield, the first station north of Derby on the main line, and takes in the whole of the former Wirksworth branch and its steep extension up to Ravenstor. The latter line terminates a short walk away from the High Peak Trail which was formerly the Cromford & High Peak Railway. The EVLR held a steam event on 6 and 7 May 2013 in which a GWR 0-6-2T worked the branch trains between Wirksworth and Duffield. Two Barclay 0-4-0STs also had duties, this one giving brake van rides up and down a long siding at Wirksworth. Its driver had a sense of the dramatic because, each time his very short train came through the bridge just before the station, he would open wide the regulator and cylinder drain cocks of No. 3, with this photogenic result.

OPPOSITE: A difficult challenge was how to take any photographs that reflected some of the atmosphere of excitement when the six surviving A4 Pacifics were gathered round one side of the turntable in the National Railway Museum at York. On 10 July 2013, I struggled to find any view of the locomotives that was not blocked by the hordes of visitors that thronged around the turntable in front of all six streamliners; the crowds can be seen at the top of this photograph. This view of 60009 *Union of South Africa*, obtained by looking down from the footbridge in the main hall, was the only one that gave a clear view of anything. It actually looks down into the tender coal space, and through into the locomotive's cab. This wide angle image also shows the Pullman-type gangway at the back of the corridor tender that was once used to enable the engine crews to change over mid-way on a London to Edinburgh non-stop run; it also shows the narrowing of the coal space on the right where the side corridor encroaches on it, a view that will possibly be of use to certain locomotive modellers. It is this sort of challenge that forces photographers to push their artistic boundaries!

It is not often that a diesel locomotive on five coaches makes an image that is more special than average, but I like this one for several reasons. The scene is at Peja station in Kosovo on 10 May 2014, with the mountains that border Albania in the background. The locomotive is a recently overhauled former Yugoslav Railways' General Motors diesel electric A1A-A1A, brought back to useful condition in the Czech Republic, carrying Kosovo Railways fleet number 001. The five matching smartly-turned-out coaches are part of a group of carriages that were donated by Austria when Kosovo was recovering from its war damage after the NATO countries had forced Serbia to withdraw and allow Kosovo to govern itself. The railway had also received locomotives from other countries, particularly Norway, and diesel railcars from Sweden. A well-publicised aid train even travelled all the way from Great Britain to Prishtina, the capital, hauled by two Class 20s. So this image is poignant, pleasant to look at, and a memory of a very enjoyable trip organised by Ffestiniog Travel; I have no connection with that company other than as a very satisfied customer.

On the same tour with Ffestiniog Travel, we visited the small and delightful country of Macedonia, which once was one of the semi-autonomous republics inside Yugoslavia.. While changing from train to a coach at Kičevo station in readiness for a journey to the once-remote Lake Ohrid, we espied this 600mm gauge train plinthed in the middle of the road outside the station. This train was from the former Lake Ohrid Railway in which passengers used to suffer for eighteen hours on wooden seats to cover the one hundred and sixty-seven kilometres from Gostivar to Ohrid. The railway had closed in 1967, and I was unaware that any stock had survived, so you can imagine my excitement at seeing this! The locomotive is a standard German *Feldbahn* 0-8-0T, and the coaches appear to be unique to the Ohrid railway. I do like the striking image and colours of the Macedonian flag that was flying by the train, so I have emphasised these by adjusting the photograph in Photoshop Elements so that the flag remains in colour but the rest of the photograph is rendered in monochrome.

Visiting Llandudno in North Wales in spring 2015, Mary and I enjoyed a ride on the Great Orme Tramway, previously the Great Orme Railway. This is in two rope-worked sections, the ropes being laid in a slot between the rails. There are winding engines at the half-way and summit stations. Passengers have to transfer between cars at the half-way point. On the lower, urban section, car 5 comes quietly up through the narrow roads, with an ever-widening view of Llandudno bay behind it. This view is late in the day when the uphill trams were almost empty but the downhill trams were busy bringing tourists back from the Great Orme headland.

Looking across towards Snowdonia we watched tram 4 leave the Great Orme summit station and pass the remains of an old quarry that now blends into the landscape. There are several good walks signposted around the headland, well worth the exercise on a dry, sunny day. If only more days there could be as bright and sunny as this one! With this composition, there is a great danger that the green part of the scene might appear cut off from the blue part by the strong diagonal boundary line. Hopefully, the perceived relationship between land and sea is close enough to prevent this.

Sometimes a picture hits a photographer as he or she walks around. This was one such case, the scene that faced us as we alighted at Salzburg, Austria, from our RailJet train in which we had travelled from Munich in summer 2016. The bright red ÖBB 'Taurus' Bo-Bo 1116.063 with its smart inter-city coaches stood out from the white surroundings of the modern station; the awning supports helped to frame the scene. Mary waited patiently alongside me as I took the picture. This station design is a huge contrast to the more traditional one in the next picture.

ABOVE: In 2015, Mary and I visited Malta for the first time. Then we took the ferry to Sicily, and travelled by train to Taormina, a hill town with a famous ancient Greek theatre and a view across to Mount Etna. Taormina station was looking smart and pristine, so I took this picture on our arrival while Mary walked towards the exit. The locomotive is one of TrenItalia's Bo+Bo+Bo articulated electric locomotives, 654.454, and the train is bound for Rome via the Messina train ferry. Photoshop was essential to lighten the tones under the platform awning and at the side of the train. Using the 'Feather' facility meant that the adjustment did not leave any visible edge to the adjusted areas.

LEFT: Later the same year we travelled to Romania where two friends had arranged a holiday tour for us in return for some critical medical help one of them had received in the UK. The tour included a visit to the one remaining active forestry railway in Romania, that in the province of Maramureş that starts out from Vişeu de Sus and heads up the river valley through heavily forested areas. Early in the morning, at the depot at Vişeu, 760mm-gauge 0-8-0T *Bavaria* is being prepared to work the 09:00 tourist train. A worker is loading logs into the cab while the fire takes hold. In the background is a yellow diesel locomotive that was used later that day to work a heavy timber train – all four diesels that I saw on this system were painted in different colours.

The year 2016 saw Mary and me in Romania again, but only because we had first visited Moldova to tick the box in my list of countries not yet visited. Once more, this was with Ffestiniog Travel, another tour advertised as 'pushing the boundaries' to less-well-visited countries. Returning through eastern Romania, the tour included a couple of days in the Moldoviţa area visiting one of Bucovina's painted monasteries as well as riding the tourist railway out of Moldoviţa itself. The day after riding the train, the party had the opportunity to follow the train along the roadside railway that had once carried thousands of tonnes of timber through lovely scenery. Just before the train approached this vantage point, a white van drew up at the side of the road – yes, they even have 'white van men' in eastern Europe! – which I subsequently cut out of the photograph by enlarging just the part of the image around the train. My trusty Sony DSLR produced enough pixels, sharpness and image depth to make this an easy adjustment; only half the original image area is displayed here.

Nokia Lumia mobile phone camera

LEFT: Until September 2014 I always used my Sony Alpha 200 DSLR camera on a tripod for photographing models on the Famous Trains model railway in Derby. When trustee Peter Swift placed on the track his scratch-built model of the LMS 1938 articulated diesel train, all I had with me was my previous mobile phone, a basic Nokia. So I took the train's photograph with the built-in camera. This is the result, which surprised me considerably. I was impressed particularly with the depth of focus, since the model train is sharp from end to end. Also, the colour rendering is lifelike, and the ability to enlarge the image to A4 size is proven. From then on, nearly all my model pictures have been taken on mobile phone cameras. The next few photographs are also results from mobile phone cameras.

BELOW: When visiting London in 2012, I wanted to test the Nokia's camera in unpromising lighting conditions, such as in a London Underground station. I alighted from a Bakerloo Line train at Waterloo before heading off to a meeting, and had planned to get a shot of the underground train before it left. It had just started moving when my mobile's camera shutter fired, and yet the image is sharp.

For a railway enthusiast to visit the National Railway Museum at York without a camera sounds stupid! But I did that in 2012 while in the city for other reasons. Happily, my Nokia's camera was up to the task. This smart line-up shows, right to left, the record-breaking A4 *Mallard*, alongside the LMS streamliner *Duchess of Hamilton*, with Gresley's V2 *Green Arrow* on the left. In the extreme left background is 35029 *Ellerman Lines*, the 'Merchant Navy' 4-6-2 that is displayed in cut-away format so that generations of enthusiasts can see how a steam locomotive works.

Microsoft Lumia 640 smartphone camera
LEFT: By October 2015, on the large 00-scale model railway at Famous Trains in Derby, stopping trains were able to stop at Chinley station automatically using equipment installed by Heathcote Electronics. This photograph was taken to promote this facility on Famous Trains' Facebook page. It shows in the foreground a Hornby 'Patriot' 4-6-0 stopped with a train for Sheffield as a Bachmann Hughes 'Crab' 2-6-0 approaches with a stopping train for Manchester. In the background a Hornby 'Britannia' approaches with the Down 'Palatine' express, and is about to pass a Heljan Metro-Vick Co-Bo leaving with a London train. The file notes tell that the exposure was 1/50th at f/2.2 with the phone's camera set at ISO250. Pretty good depth of focus for f/2.2, eh?

BELOW: A mobile phone camera can catch a lot of detail in a model close-up, as seen in this 2017 study of a two-car diesel multiple unit on the approach to Darley Green terminus at Famous Trains. The two telegraph poles do lean like that, rather prototypical perhaps?

On 1 June 2015, I noticed new 'artwork' at St. Pancras station, namely a second clock based in design and size on the main station clock but in reversed tones. I only had my mobile phone with me, and this is the result. It bears very close comparison with the DSLR picture of the similar scene early in this chapter.

This fabulously-tiled hall is not, as you might expect, in a stately home somewhere. It is the entrance hall at São Bento station, the main terminus in the centre of the fine city of Porto in northern Portugal. The hall's architectural splendour is capped by the two words moulded and highlighted on the decorative ceiling: 'Minho' and 'Douro'. These are the two significant rivers after which the early railway here was named, the Caminhos de Ferro Estado Minho e Douro. When the passenger in the bright red jacket walked across my view as I took this photograph, I cursed under my breath, and took another one without him, which is the picture I originally wanted. However, I think his bright red jacket contrasts wonderfully with the blue and brown tiles on the walls, and he has placed himself bang on one of the thirds, so he stays! The decorative wall tiles are fine examples of Portugal's ceramic art known as *azulejos*, an attractive feature of many stations and other buildings across the country, even quite modest ones.

TECHNIQUES IN FILM PHOTOGRAPHY

It may surprise many older readers to realise that several of the youngest readers of this book will never have used a film camera, having been brought up in the digital world. In the same way, I have never used a plate camera, having been born into a world that could access films for photography. Other, more senior photographers will have used films for most of their lives, and some may, even now, be resisting the change to digital photography. These two Appendices therefore are aimed at clarifying for each group of railway photographers the techniques used by the other group. I also try to highlight the advantages and disadvantages of each. I do not discuss plate cameras at any length as I have no experience of them.

I transferred to digital photography partially in 2002 and totally in 2004. I have never used a film since early that year. So, my recollection of how I did things before then may be slightly hazy, though I hope not seriously so.

I know some photographers who stick to film photography, specifically colour slides, because they say the quality of the projected image is higher than is obtained by digital projection. That is possibly true; in fact, it is probably the *only* advantage of film photography over what can now be achieved digitally. But there are so many other advantages of digital photography that I believe overshadow any benefit there may be in sticking with films or slides.

There are in effect two main threads of film photography, that are significantly different from each other. These use either negatives from which prints are made, or colour slides.

Negative film photography

Photography using negative films or plates which are then printed on photographic paper meets the needs of many people who like to have their efforts displayed in albums or framed for viewing as pictures hung on walls, or enlarged to poster size or bigger as promotional displays. Techniques vary depending on how much the photographer wants to be involved in the process. In my case, for black-and-white photography I developed my own films and printed them in my darkroom, simply because I held the, occasionally mistaken, belief that I could get better results that way than by submitting them to a shop or laboratory for processing. However, for colour photography I baulked at the added complications in the processes and always had my films developed and printed commercially.

Before my time, several well-known railway photographers such as Maurice W. Earley and O.J. Morris used large glass plates in their cameras instead of film. This was because they could create sharper and less grainy photographs that way. Their cameras were cumbersome and needed tripods to stand on. A swing-back facility on the camera enabled the photographer to focus along the train, making it sharp from front to back. A standard fixed-back camera has a field of focus roughly at right angles to the centreline of the lens. With more modern, smaller negative sizes, the depth of focus is much greater, so it is easier to stop down enough to keep the train sharp.

The larger plate sizes had one innate advantage over films. They could be used to create large contact prints, not using an enlarger. Contact printing was the surest way to get really sharp prints.

When I look back I am amazed that, when I returned from a long tour, such as my trip to Ireland in 1957, I would spend several successive weekend mornings in my darkroom developing perhaps two or four films each time until I had worked my way through them all. Then I spent the same time on subsequent weekends printing them. There was no such thing as good quality instant-results photography in those days!

Developing films

Developing films was fairly straightforward. In complete darkness, not even with a safety light lit, one had to thread the film into the grooves of the spool that would then be placed in the developing tank. Sweaty fingers could cause the film to stick on its way into the grooves, so life was not always simple! After the tank's lid was properly in place, which rendered the film safe in the darkness inside, we could switch the room light on or regain daylight. We would choose a developer from the many on sale in the local photo shop. I chose fine-grain developers such as Microdol, Promicrol and Acutol. One had to mix the developer with water and warm it to the correct temperature, measured to be within +/- one degree of the figure stated in the developer instruction leaflet. Then we poured the developer into the tank and left it there for the designated time, with the tank standing in warm water to maintain the developer temperature. The tank had a spool driver rod that enabled one to turn the spool once or twice every

minute to keep the developer properly mixed. Too little developing time, and the image would be thin; too long and the image would be thick, contrasty and possibly grainy. A small thermometer dropped down the centre hole of the tank would enable the photographer to check on the temperature which had to be maintained within close limits. After pouring out the developer I always followed it with an acid stop bath made up of diluted acetic acid, though some people would use plain water. This also had to be at the correct temperature. Then one poured in the fixer, which would convert the developed image grains into silver grains which would be permanent. Again, the temperature had to be right to prevent any image distortion. Thankfully, after all this the process of washing the film for twenty minutes or so to remove all chemical traces was not temperature-critical. Then the film would be hung up to dry. I used to cut the dried film into individual negatives for large format or strips of six for 35mm, for storage in the album envelopes. Some people still do all this now.

I have to admit that I did not enjoy film developing; I regarded it as a necessary part of the process. My enjoyment came in producing good quality prints from these negatives.

Printing from black-and-white negatives

In my darkroom I had two enlargers, one which could hold large format negatives and one for 35mm. The philosophy was that an enlarger lens had to be of a higher quality than the lens on the camera, otherwise there would be a loss of quality. Why have a top range camera and then dilute the image quality with a cheap enlarger lens? A speaker at a photographic society once said that having a cheap enlarger lens was like buying a Rolls-Royce and running it on paraffin!

There was commonality between the film development process and that for prints. Each employed a developer, stopper and fixer, and each required the output to be washed and then dried. The fun came with what was done with the image projected in the enlarger from the negative onto the paper held in the frame on the base. The process required the darkroom to be dark, lit only with a red darkroom lamp; black-and-white photographic paper was/is formulated to have no response to red light, only white. Before putting paper in the frame, the image was composed within the frame to the size and angle required, and the lens moved up and down to focus the image to be sharp. The enlarger lens iris could be stopped down to make more certain that the image was sharp – I write all this in the past tense because I have not done this for twenty years!

After the image had been composed and the enlarger lamp switched off, the paper was put into the frame and the enlarger lamp lit for the required number of seconds' exposure. How many? Experience usually gave a clue, but some photographers went to the effort of producing timed test strips to select the best time for a full tone image. A thick, over-exposed negative would need more print exposure than a thin one, for example.

The fun bit was trying to darken the sky tones, or lighten the dark areas under locomotive valances, and so forth. This was done by 'shading'. To bring up the sky tones, for example, after exposing for the main picture one covered the main subject area, perhaps with one's hand or a piece of card, and exposed the sky area for a second or so more. Or one inserted the hand or card a second or two before the main picture was fully exposed so that the dark areas received less exposure. Often one needed several attempts on several sheets of paper before getting the right effect. It is so much easier with

digital printing – see Appendix 2. I found it almost impossible to produce from one negative repeat prints that looked the same when finished.

Most paper manufacturers sold around five contrast grades as well as papers with different surfaces – glossy, matt, eggshell, for example – and of different sizes such as postcard, half-plate, whole-plate, 10in x 8in, etc. The photographer had to assess the contrast of the negative being printed, and choose a contrast grade paper that matched it. For example, a negative with correct contrast needed 'normal' grade paper; a flat (soft) negative needed a 'hard' (more contrasty) paper to compensate for the lack of contrast; a contrasty negative needed a 'soft' paper, and so on. Negatives at the extremes of contrast or flatness needed either 'extra soft' or 'extra hard', and good results were often difficult to achieve with these because the exposure latitude of these papers was relatively small.

One firm produced Multigrade paper to offset the cost of storing up to five contrast grades of printing paper. This required the photographer to insert a filter below the enlarger lens, each filter representing a different contrast grade. The results I saw were quite good, but never completely sparkling, so I did not try that technique for myself.

Printing papers would be developed in a tray and if the exposure had been correct the image would begin to emerge after a few seconds; the photographer would allow it to reach full development. If the exposure under the enlarger was too long, the image would come up too quickly; whipping the paper out of the developer early to stop development would usually produce a muddy image. Equally, too short an exposure time would produce an image that failed to reach its full density. Under the gloom of a red safelight I often found it difficult to judge when the print quality was at its best.

The next tray would contain either water or a stop bath; for the stop bath I used diluted acetic acid which some chemist shop owners made me sign for in the Poisons Book! The fixer was in the third tray, after which the prints would go to be washed under running tap water. Temperature control during printing was not critical, though developers would perform better if not too cold. After washing, the prints had to be hung up to dry. Some people would then take their glossy prints, and glaze them on a shiny heated metal sheet. I used to do that, but when family pressures reduced my available time I dispensed with that chore. An unglazed gloss print was good enough for most purposes including publishing.

Other techniques

Removing unwanted things like lampposts sticking out of steam locomotive chimneys was difficult, though not impossible. If one's eyesight was good enough, one could paint a special photographic dye, usually red, over the offending image, carefully avoiding covering any part of the picture that one wanted to show on the print. Then the negative could be printed, but it was necessary to make the print contrasty so that the sky area came out dead white, otherwise the dye would show up as a white ghost image in the sky.

Removing negative scratches or spots required adept use of a small paintbrush and some artist's watercolour black paint, applied with care to the final, dried print surface.

Removing converging verticals was more difficult and required the paper frame to be tilted upwards toward the enlarger so that the convergence was corrected. This would slightly elongate the image, and I knew of no way to correct that, so judgement was needed as to how far to make the correction. One snag was that the enlarger lens needed to be stopped down heavily to keep the print in focus over its full depth. This would not only affect the exposure time, but also make the image more difficult to see when focussing. I think I tried this process only once or twice.

Colour slides

There are some fundamental differences between using negative films and films for colour slides. While a negative is the definitive source of future images, it is not what the normal viewer sees. Photographs from negatives are only normally viewed after printing, little else. With colour slides, on the other hand, the developed film image is both the definitive image and also the picture seen by the viewer, either through a magnifier or a projector. Lose the slide and you have lost the source of the image. It is possible to make or buy duplicates of your slides. Some are pretty good, though none can ever be as good as the original. That is partly because the duplicate slide is made on another colour slide film, not necessarily the same make or grade as the original. Minor differences in colour saturation and hue can affect duplicates; rarely are they as sharp as the originals, based on my experience with commercial copy slides. As I wrote above, the differences may be quite marginal, and for projection, duplicate slides may be of sufficient quality. However, if the photographer has moved on to digital projection, the slides to be projected can be scanned and converted to digital files, ready for inclusion in a digital slide show.

In taking photographs on slide film, the photographer has to bear in mind certain restraints. A colour slide film has less exposure latitude than a negative film. An under-exposed slide looks dark on the screen when projected and shadow detail may be blocked out. An over-exposed slide looks pale, and may bleach out some of the brighter detail. So, exposures for colour slides must be right.

Whereas with black-and-white negative photography some people slightly over expose to be sure of getting all the shadow tones on the negative, on a colour slide this can be fatal, perhaps leaving no detail in the sky. Again, I stress, colour slides must be exposed correctly, if possible to within half a stop of ideal each time. I had my camera shutter tested on a couple of occasions and found that, whereas the lower shutter speeds were correct, the fastest were a bit slow; 1/300th second for example came out at 1/175th, a difference of almost one stop. Thus, I risked over-exposure when using a faster shutter speed. Just a thought – why not get your shutter tested?

Slide shows of railways are still very popular among members of the UK's many railway societies. It is important when preparing a show using slides to bear in mind the performance of the projector that will be used. Many projectors have a form of automatic focusing, and this helps to take care of the different thicknesses of slide mounts, as well as the tendency of the slides to 'pop' when warmed by the projector lamp. A projector with just manual focus can be a pain to manage during a long slide show, particularly if the slides come from several different sources and thin and thick mounts are mixed up among the collection being shown. Preparation should include placing the slides in magazines, the right way round and the right way up, and in the order in which the projector will show them. Check this is all right before loading a hundred or more slides; you cannot just turn a magazine round if you get the format wrong!

Storage
Black-and-white negatives that are on films based on silver compounds are permanent and can be printed a century later if stored well. Those based on colour film technology need greater care. They

should ideally always be kept inside the house at room temperature. Do not be tempted ever to store negatives and slides in the garage or loft. Damp conditions can encourage growth of interesting fungus patterns on films, and these can rarely be properly removed when discovered decades later. Always store negatives in proper photographic envelopes or sleeves, never in ordinary postal or other envelopes which may chemically affect the images.

If negatives are stored properly, it almost does not matter what happens to stored prints because they can always be replaced. Stored slides that deteriorate are as good as lost, so keep them carefully indoors and away from any light. Some slide boxes are translucent, so be careful not to keep them where light can get at them. Put them in a big box, or in a cupboard with no glass windows.

Finding them again
You will need to find your negatives or slides later on, believe me. Do not think that you will always remember where they are, or in which box a particular photograph sits. As the years go by your pictures may amass to surprisingly large numbers; I gave up counting when I passed 20,000 and may have over 30,000 negatives and slides now. And as the years go by your memory will change as life's other priorities take precedence over what you thought you knew twenty or more years ago.

Catalogue your pictures. Methods for this are numerous. You can list them in books, keep a database on your computer, it almost does not matter so long as you can quickly find a picture years later when you need to. From 1954 to 1984 my black-and-white photographs were kept as postcard prints in boxes relating to their subject matter. Each print had the negative number written in ink on the back. The negative number was that which I had written on the sheet in the negative album that held the negative. So, I can take out the box of BR diesel locomotives for example, find the picture I want – say of a Class 47 – read the negative number, go to the album that contains that negative and, hey presto, I have got the negative inside a minute or so.

It's not as easy for me with slides. My colour slides are all in boxes labelled by the year they were taken. Unless I can remember the year I took a slide, I have to trail through all the boxes around the most likely year. Remember there are up to thirty-six slides in a box and I might have taken a dozen or more boxes of slides in any year. I just wish I had made lists of my slides! Since 1997, I catalogued in Access on my computer, databases of slides, negatives and digital images that I have taken from that time. I can find anything quickly with a computer search. And don't forget to back it up (see Appendix 2).

The first camera that I could call my own was a standard Brownie box camera. This took 120-size roll film. This picture shows a similar camera of a different make. On my camera, for 'instantaneous' exposures the shutter lever was pulled over once, giving an exposure time reckoned by the makers to be about 1/25th second. After winding on to the next negative, the shutter lever could be moved across in the opposite direction to take the next photo, again once only. The lens was fixed; there was no focus adjustment, and no means of increasing or reducing the amount of light reaching the film. There was no interlock between the shutter and the film winder, so it was very possible, if one forgot to wind on the film, to take two photographs on one negative, otherwise called 'double-exposure'. There was a metal knob to wind on the film. My type of box camera was made by Brownie from 1900 to the early 1960s. (*Internet*)

This photograph shows a similar box camera of another make. With the camera back withdrawn, it illustrates the principle of how the roll film was wrapped round the outside of the camera's inside frame. The numbers on the backing paper show through two small red windows in the camera body so that, when the photographer winds on the film, he or she can stop winding when the number of the next negative appears in the window. A large format camera such as the Brownie box camera took eight 3¼in x 2¼in images in a film length. The higher numbers printed on the backing paper relate to when the film is loaded in a different type of camera sized for sixteen images on a 120-size film, where the small windows are at a different position.

This is the Nagel Librette folding camera with which I took my first railway photographs, and which I had on permanent loan from my father from 1953. It was made in the period between 1928 and 1931 after Dr August Nagel had set up his own factory in Stuttgart, Germany, after having resigned from his previous employment with Zeiss; he sold his factory to Kodak in 1931. The folding camera had a good lens based on Zeiss technology, a Compur shutter with a top speed of 1/250th second, and both a prismatic viewfinder and a wire frame one. The wire frame and its eye-piece are prominent in the picture. At the time of publication of this book, the camera is ninety years old and still in working order!

When I bought my Zeiss Super-Ikonta 532/16 camera, I had high hopes of its performance and I was not disappointed. The lens quality was excellent, the shutter able to reach 1/300th second and the see-through viewfinder was easy to use. The 2¼ inch square format enabled any photograph to be used in horizontal or vertical format, or both, and if the whole square picture area was printed, the field of view was startling. I did some of my best work with this camera. Its only disadvantage was that the winding mechanism spaced the negatives a little further apart than standard, and so it could only take eleven pictures on one 120 film, not twelve like other square-format cameras. (*Alf Sigaro*)

This 35mm Voitländer Vito IIa folding camera was so convenient, I used it for colour slides from 1959 to 1986. The f/3.5 Color-Skopar lens was advertised to have been specially formulated to give accurate colours with no colour cast. The Prontor shutter had up to 1/300th second speeds. The camera took at least thirty-six pictures on a cassette of film, and could be carried easily in a pocket, it was so compact when folded. When required, this camera also performed better in black-and-white than the more expensive Periflex 3 which I had bought in 1962.

The Corfield Periflex 3 was meant to be the UK's answer to the world-famous Leica 35mm camera but at a more affordable price. However, mine proved a disappointment. True, it did take some very good photographs, at least six of them good enough to be included in this book. But the particular camera's slightly untrue focal plane meant that sharpness was not consistent across the photograph when the lens was at or near full aperture. The facility of an f/2 lens was one reason why I bought the camera in the first place; I had wanted to use Ilford's excellent fine grain Pan F film and a large-aperture lens was essential to cater for that film's slow speed of 50ASA. The camera's more serious fault was the focal plane shutter, a clever device in which two 'curtains' raced across the frame, the distance between them giving the required shutter speed. In my camera, the two halves sometimes closed up on each other, rendering one part of the picture darker than the rest. Occasionally they came together part-way across, leaving the rest of the picture blank – totally unacceptable. When I sent the camera away the third time for the manufacturer's attention to these faults, the retailer lent me a Periflex 2 for the duration; this also had the same shutter fault. That convinced me to sell the Periflex, the money from which came in handy for Mary and me to buy our first dining room table! (*Internet*)

Five years after selling the Periflex, I could afford another camera. A photographic shop in Cardiff where we lived at the time had a good-condition second-hand German-made Rollei 35 for sale for £70. This proved to be an excellent purchase. It was the first camera I had owned that had a built-in exposure meter, which substantially simplified judging exposures. Its 40mm lens had a wider field of view than many standard lenses, and produced some very sharp images. I had settled on FP4 film by then because the maximum aperture of this camera, as well as my colour camera, was f/3.5 and that suited a 100ASA film better than one limited to 50ASA. With the lens retracted into the body, the camera could easily fit into a pocket, it was so compact. This delightful instrument gave me good service for black-and-white photography for fifteen years.

In 1985, I purchased my first proper SLR camera, a Minolta X-300. Minolta lenses were acknowledged to be among the best in the industry, and this one's 50mm standard lens was no exception. It gave very sharp black-and-white pictures. The Minolta shutter would reach 1/1000th second, the camera was well balanced and easy to handle, the viewfinder very clear to see through, and its built-in exposure meter enabled automatic exposure setting if I wanted it. I followed this purchase with a Tamron 70mm to 150mm zoom lens so as to bring distant subjects closer, and later another that covered 28mm to 70mm, at which point the Minolta standard 50mm lens had frequent rests. Then I bought a second X-300 for colour slides, and that was excellent, too. I shared the two zoom and the standard lens between the two cameras. These remained my workaday cameras until I went digital in 2004. One got stolen from our house around 2002, and I replaced it with a second-hand X-300, not needing anything more complicated.

Just for the record, since I showed a picture earlier on of a size 120 roll film in a box camera, here is a typical 35mm film cassette. Unlike the roll film which is protected by its long backing paper at each end, the 35mm film has to be rewound into the cassette when fully exposed. Changing cassettes in the camera is then simplicity itself.

ABOVE LEFT: For developing films, a developing tank is needed that has a central spool and a lid that keeps the light out, as well as a central turning rod and, preferably, a cap to enable the tank to be turned over without spilling any of the liquid inside it. Some tanks have double spools, so that two films can be developed at once. They can still be purchased on line if you really want one. (*Internet*)

ABOVE RIGHT: When producing prints, I used three trays similar to these, one each for developer, acid wash and fixer. Mine were able to take 10in x 8in papers lying flat. These trays are on display in the darkroom in the basement of Eltham Palace in south London.

LEFT: My Durst enlarger sat in my darkroom in the loft of our house. One could raise and lower the enlarger head to alter the size of the image projected on the base or frame (not shown). This enlarger enabled smaller height adjustments to be made for detailed sharpening, if one's ageing eyes could see the difference. In an article in the *Railway Magazine* I mentioned that I had this enlarger for disposal. Out of the magazine's 30,000-plus readers, no-one came forward to have it! It sadly ended up in a skip. Digital photography had already eclipsed this sort of thing.

DIGITAL RAILWAY PHOTOGRAPHY

In 2002, I needed to replace my desktop computer. I went to PC World who were selling a package for photographers. This centred on a computer of the specification I wanted, sold with a flatbed scanner and a basic digital 'compact' camera thrown in, together with a disk containing Adobe Photoshop 5 Limited Edition. This is the set-up that got me going in digital photography.

The camera was nothing special, just a fixed-lens Fuji camera capable of recording two million pixels per image, a digital equivalent to a box camera. Actually, two million pixels capability is not much. It is equivalent to a coarse grained film such as Ilford HP5 used to be. I had already calculated that, for the performance of a digital camera to equal the average SLR film camera, it would need to create an image with at least ten million pixels. There were one or two cameras around in the early 2000s that could do that, but on sale for over £1,000, unaffordable at the time. However, the Fuji digital camera was just small enough for me to keep in my briefcase, and I did indeed use it for the odd photograph that would otherwise go unrecorded. I quickly discovered that, if used within its limitations, prints from this camera were acceptable up to A5 size. Indeed, one such print from this camera was published in the magazine *Modern Railways* as a half-page article header in 2003, and looked perfectly okay. The modern standard paper size A5 is roughly equivalent to the once-popular Whole Plate size of photographic paper which was 8½in x 6½in. A6 is slightly narrower

than Postcard. A4 size, at 11.69in x 8.27in, is slightly larger than the old 10in x 8in photo paper.

I surmised that I could produce A4 sized pictures if I could get a digital camera that could produce at least five million pixels in an image. This came about in 2004 when I bought my first digital SLR camera, a Konica-Minolta A1. Again, the results were very good if I did not push the boundaries too far. Indeed, photographs from this camera were good enough for me to abandon films for good. The only disadvantage that I found with this camera was the positioning of the many buttons around its body; I accidentally pressed several of them by mistake when handling the camera, which made for some interesting results on occasions!

My current DSLR camera and also my mobile phone camera produces ten million pixels which is enough for me for the time being. More modern cameras can now go as far as twenty or twenty-four million pixels, which has considerable other advantages that I will explain later. Each of my digital SLRs had a settings wheel which could be turned to enable the camera to set itself to the type of photograph one was taking. For example, in addition to Auto, in which the camera works things out for itself, there is Programme which keeps your own exposure and quality settings, Scene which sets the camera for landscape pictures, Action which sets the shutter for faster speed and larger aperture, and Sunset which knocks out the effect of the automatic colour balance that would otherwise whiten out the red glow of the sun at dusk. Mine has Shutter Priority and Aperture Priority settings, too. There are other settings depending on a particular camera manufacturer's policy.

The method one uses for processing digital pictures depends on individual needs. Many shops can make prints from digital images, usually the same shops that used to handle developing and printing from films. They can usually process images delivered to them on camera memory cards, or on CD or DVD disks, or on computer memory sticks. Some may well allow you to email the images directly to them.

Interestingly, firms that still make prints from negative films or colour slides are almost exclusively scanning and printing them digitally. Wet printing is out!

Scanning photographs

It is possible easily to scan photographs from negatives, prints or slides, be they colour or black-and-white, and produce fine grain digital images from all of them if the originals themselves are not grainy! There are two key types of scanner.

Flatbed scanners

Good flatbed scanners are not horrendously expensive and are usually able to scan any paper document or photographic print up to A4 size. Many flatbed scanners have adaptors that can also convert them to negative or slide scanners, though in most cases the final image resolution is lower than would come from a custom 35mm slide or film scanner.

The scanner has to be connected to a computer that has appropriate scanning software on it. Some quite acceptable software can now be downloaded free from the internet. The software can include image adjustments that take care of differences in, for example, colour balance, tone range, brightness, etc. Through the

software, the user should set the scanner for a resolution figure that will give a file size of at least ten megabytes, JPEG file, if a large print size is required. For example, if I am to print a picture at its original size on my printer which prints at three hundred dots per inch, I set the scanner to three hundred dots per inch or more. I discuss in the next section what to do with this file once it is saved on the computer. A JPEG file attempts to compress the image, usually by joining up neighbouring pixels of about the same colour and intensity. This keeps the file size reasonable, and most viewers do not notice any deterioration of the image. This book is full of JPEGs. If you do not want this compression, then use a file type such as TIFF; the file size will be up three or more times as big, however, and will take up that much more memory; it also takes more time to process.

A good quality flatbed scanner often has a plastic film carrier that enables the scanner to hold negatives and slides for scanning. I use my flatbed scanner for negatives of 3¼in x 2¼in size, or 2¼in square, and I set the scanner at 1,200 dots per inch which produces a big enough file size. My current flatbed scanner is an Epson Perfection 4490 Photo scanner. The software I use is that supplied by the scanner manufacturer. This has amateur and professional settings. I use the professional settings because that gives me much more control over the image quality, but the amateur settings are fine if the photographs being scanned are of consistent quality. All the early black-and-white images in this book have been scanned in my Epson scanner at the professional setting.

35mm film and slide scanners

35mm film and slide scanners are much more expensive than flatbed scanners and there is not at present a great deal of choice at the more affordable end of the market. My first slide scanner was by Minolta. When that broke down, Konica, who had taken over Minolta, showed no interest in repairing it. So, I bought one from Nikon for about £300 – I said they were more expensive! Nikon scanners are currently less easily obtainable in the UK, so I now have a much cheaper one from plustek which performs well. It actually performs better with a free software called VueScan which I downloaded from the internet. The software it came with did not help scanning dark areas which came out magenta in hue when they should have been black. VueScan does not do that, thankfully, and is much easier to manage.

35mm film and slide scanners use different feeder trays to run slides or films through the scanner, and the images are scanned one at a time which can be time-consuming. Again, the software enables you to set the scanner for colour or black-and-white, negative or positive, and there are some adjustments such as for colour balance, contrast, brightness, sharpness and output file type. Each scan can be set differently for any individual image depending on its density, contrast and colour balance.

The film and slide scanners I have used do produce very large files because they are capable of recording images at very high resolution. This is usually so good that any grain or scratches on the original negative or slide are faithfully recorded! The scanner software usually includes a sharpening feature that can improve the sharpness of the image by gently highlighting the edge contrast between adjacent tones.

It is not necessary to make the tone or colour corrections perfect at this stage because these can be fully adjusted after the image is saved on the computer (see below). What is important when scanning is to make sure that all the tones on the slide or negative are there – that there are no bleached highlights or blocked shadows, for example. If these features exist on the original image, however, there is little that can be done about them. But

if they are introduced on the scan, there is nothing you can do to correct them later without rescanning.

It is thus possible to hold photographic images on a computer that were originally black-and-white negatives, colour slides, colour negatives or from a digital camera. All of these images can be fed into one album, or one digital slide show, or displayed on any digital media. They can be sent via the internet to diverse locations around the world, or to publishers, avoiding the need to part company ever again with one's precious original slides or negatives.

And a flatbed scanner connected to a computer with a printer attached enables anyone to photo-copy documents without leaving the house – I just thought you would like to know that!

Image adjustment

As an equivalent to the diverse darkroom techniques for adjusting tones in photographs, some of which I described in Appendix 1, the potential for image adjustment on computers is vast. There are many different makes of software that perform these operations well. Some are horrendously expensive for amateur use, including the current versions of the professional suite of Adobe Photoshop. Thankfully, Adobe also produces Photoshop Elements which is very much more affordable; I use it and find it has all the features I need plus a lot that I may never use. I bought Photoshop Elements 9, though the latest is version 15 which says it can cure the blurring effect of camera shake. I have yet to try that.

The big difference when digital photography is compared with film photography is that colour slides, once scanned, can have image adjustments applied; this was never previously possible with professionally developed slides. Thus, a slightly over-exposed colour slide can be turned into a satisfactory, full-tone image, so long as all the details of the subject are still present on the slide. Under-exposed slides can also be rescued, though they do tend to be more grainy due to the thicker layers on the slide, and shadow detail may be lacking.

Simple things that image-adjustment software can do include:

- Straightening up a picture on the slant;
- Cropping a photo to eliminate unwanted background/foreground, etc.;
- Resizing an image to make it big enough to print, or small enough to post on the internet, or the right size to put in a slide show using Powerpoint, say;
- Setting contrast;
- Setting colour balance.

For a railway photographer, there are other image adjustments that can prove extremely useful. One combination of features enables a photographer to lighten the very dark area that occurs below a steam locomotive footplate or valance, or a station awning or roof, particularly when the sunlight is strong. In these circumstances, the detail in the shadows is often almost blocked out. What I do using Photoshop Elements is to highlight the shadow area, either using the 'Lasso' tool or the 'Magic Wand', and 'Feather' the edge of the selected area by up to 200 pixels. I can then apply the tone adjustment to lighten the shadow area, and if necessary adjust its contrast, so that it looks naturally lighter. The feathered edge to the adjusted area prevents there being a visually detectable edge to the adjusted area. Images from modern digital cameras of ten or more million pixels have enough detail in the shadows to enable the photographer to pull out the detail very well this way. Older colour slides usually don't have enough shadow detail for this

to be entirely successful, unfortunately, but good black-and-white negatives can often come up with the detail.

The same technique can be used to darken sky or steam exhaust areas to bring out the detail of clouds or steam, a bit like the shading we did in darkrooms decades ago. Be careful not to overdo the adjustment. There are pictures in popular railway magazines nowadays that look – to me – awful because the sky is too blue or the tones are all of the same intensity. The final result has to look natural. This is not cheating. The image on a see-through slide can be of much greater contrast and tone range than any printing paper or magazine page can reproduce accurately. Thus, image adjustment is often necessary just to bring the tone range and contrast of a slide down to that which can be printed on paper.

Photoshop and other software products can be used to cheat, if you really must! On occasions, I have been guilty of eliminating from a photograph a person wearing high-visibility clothing when it is not visually appropriate. I have not done this anywhere in the photographs in this book, with one exception admitted in the caption. The old-fashioned way is to use the airbrush facility to paint the guy out. Equally one can copy a nearby area and paste it over the offending person. The result can be complete disappearance of the offender, with no visual way of detecting that this has been done.

I do sometimes use this technique for removing unwanted lampposts and telegraph poles that stick out of steam locomotive chimneys because the photographer was blind to them at the time the picture was taken. We used to do this in the darkroom by painting dye over the unwanted item on the negative, and then printing it so that the sky was dead white, otherwise the outline of the dye would be visible as a white ghost on the print. By painting out the unwanted item on digital software, all the sky tones can be preserved.

Photoshop is capable of making sensible colour adjustments, though again this should be done with care. Under the 'Enhance' button is 'Auto Levels' which will bring the colour range in the picture to what the computer thinks is about right, eliminating any significant colour cast. This also adjusts the overall contrast to produce a full tone range. I found this useful with an old Ferrania colour slide of the little engine *Polar Bear* in the Isle of Man that had a deep magenta colour cast. The result was pretty good, and needed only a little more adjustment of colour saturation to satisfy me. On the other hand, if you do this with a picture of a sunset or a night scene, the software will try to make it look like normal daylight, so it has its limitations! The computer is not always right, but you can back-track on any changes you have made. The 'Auto Contrast' facility is also useful, but you may still need to adjust for shadows and highlights.

A new feature that was introduced with version 9 of Photoshop Elements – at least, that's when I found out about it – enabled converging verticals to be corrected. How many pictures of tall buildings look wrong to the human eye because the brain says the sides should be upright, not leaning inwards? The correction is fairly straightforward, though it involves several steps. The 'Image' button leads to 'Transform' and then to a selection that includes 'Perspective'. In that mode, the converging verticals can be corrected by dragging the top corner points of the highlighted outline on the screen. This action widens or narrows the pictures slightly, so the width correction is done using 'Transform' again and selecting 'Free Transform'. Drag the buttons on the middles of the two sides to meet the marked verticals, and the job only needs three more actions to complete. Firstly,

click on the green tick that enables the transformation to be saved, then click on 'Layers' and 'Flatten Image'. Lastly the somewhat distorted image outline can be cropped to the size and shape required.

Another fairly new tool in Photoshop Elements which I find hugely time-saving is a tool for eliminating scratches and spots which is very useful on old slides or negatives. You just 'paint' over the scratch or area to be eliminated; the computer works out what image details should replace the scratch or spot or telegraph pole, and replaces it with a usually good guess based on the tones either side of the scratch or around the spot. It will even enable you to extend the area at an edge of a picture, such as after the converging verticals procedure described above. On occasion, I have used this tool to eliminate from a picture a figure wearing high-viz clothing.

There is so much opportunity in this type of software that it is better to buy some and feel your way very slowly through it. An early tutorial can confuse. Gentle practise is by far the best educational tool for this stuff.

Printing

Printing photographs from a computer is straightforward. Just follow the instructions in the particular printer software you are using. There is also specialist software that possibly does a better job and offers more scope. My choice is Epson Easy Photoprint that came bundled with my first computer/scanner/camera combination. In this you select the pictures you want to print, decide on which printer to use and what paper quality, for example, photo quality glossy; paper size, usually A4; and how many prints you want from one A4 sheet, one, two or four. There is also scope to lighten a picture's tones if you know that your particular printer tends to print things darkly as several do – my wife's Samsung colour laser printer is a prime example. You can use this software with any make of printer.

Choice of paper is important. Some gloss papers cause ink-jet printer ink to dry slowly, leading to smudging if the surface is touched too soon; I had some Ilford paper that did that. My choice for photo printing paper is Jessops gloss paper which dries instantaneously with the printers I have used.

Some paper/ink combinations fade if a picture is left in the light for long periods. Jessops paper with ink-jet printing did that, but cheap, standard A4 document printing paper did not. So, in 2005 I bought a printer that uses pigment-inks – problem solved! A picture hung facing the window in my small study in 2005 is as colourful now, twelve years later, as it was then.

My photo printer is clever enough to print right to the edge of the paper, so a photograph can be produced with no white borders. I have always liked them that way.

If you send your negatives, slides or digital images to a shop or laboratory for printing nowadays, you will receive digitally-printed photographs. The machines they use attempt to replicate the full tone range of the image. A flat image will be printed with better contrast, and a very contrasty one may be flattened enough to be acceptable, which is good. But, if there is a dominant white sky in the image, or a bright white house in one corner, or even very bright white discs on the front of the train, the foreground subject might be printed darker than you would like because the machine will try to get some detail in the white areas. I have seen this often with members' prints submitted to the Bournemouth Railway Club's photographic portfolio to which I still contribute. The way out is to ask for the image to be processed in something like Photoshop, but that puts the cost up. It is far better to learn to make your own prints off your home computer, and it is very much more fun!

Photographs for publication

Nowadays, publishers prefer to receive photographs for publication in digital format. That makes it so much easier for the photographer than undergoing the chore of producing prints and sending them off to publishers by post, or incurring the risk of losing one's original colour slides which happened to me in the distant past, and many of which have never been returned. Nowadays, most e-mail service-providers allow quite large files to be sent as attachments. For one or two pictures, this is the best way to get your photographs to a publisher quickly, ideal if they are newsworthy. Getting the right file size is important. Most publishers are happy to receive pictures in JPEG format, and the file size must be at least 1MB, preferably around 4MB for guaranteed quality, depending on the size of the final picture in the magazine or book.

Submitting large numbers of photographs, for example to illustrate an article which may require, say, ten to twenty pictures, is better done using a specialist 'drop box' service, such as WeTransfer. These enable you to upload several large-format files to the drop box from which the recipient later downloads the images when he or she has been advised they are available.

Very large numbers of pictures, such as when submitting a book like this one with 300 illustrations for publication, necessitate putting them together either on a large capacity memory stick or on a DVD and taking or posting them to the publisher.

Mobile phones

Most modern mobile phone cameras are excellent. I no longer need to carry a camera on my travels in the UK, unless I have a very specific railway photographic exploit in mind. My low-end smartphone has a camera able to create images of ten million pixels. The lens produces sharp images and has a long field of focus such that, even when photographing a 00-scale model railway train, the train is sharp through most of its length. The mobile's ability to adjust its camera to widely different lighting conditions, particularly inside buildings or in towns at night, is very good, and the photographer need make no intervention. The only significant snags with my mobile's camera are that the touch-screen tends to be less sensitive than a normal camera shutter release, so one can sometimes have two or more goes at getting the shutter to fire; no help if the subject is moving. Also, it will not take sharp images of fast moving subjects, nor of any movement in low light. The field of view is wide angle, however, and that does not necessarily suit all railway photographic opportunities.

My mobile phone can produce images that print well up to A4 size. I have had a number of photographs from mobile phones published, with excellent results. There will always be a place for cameras, at least in my lifetime, but the mobile phone camera is certainly here to stay, and is already dominant!

Image storage

This has been a thorny issue for some time because of the changes and advances in digital storage media. From my start in 2002 through to now in 2017, I have been putting all my digital camera output images on CDs for storage. At the same time, I have stored on DVDs the larger-file images that result from being improved through Photoshop. For many years, I also used to make a good print of every photograph on the grounds that media for storing digital images may change but prints can always be scanned. This has served me well over the years. However, two things have recently changed. One is that I have learned that CDs and DVDs have a finite life and can begin to delaminate after a decade or so. Secondly

it is clear that, just as floppy disks have disappeared, so some time in the future will CDs and DVDs, and even external hard drives be superseded. Solid state storage devices are becoming more and more compact, and more people use the internet – 'the cloud' – for storing their photographs. I do not because I am averse to other people getting their hands on them! The need for keeping prints of everything has vanished.

So, I will soon have to knuckle down to copying my images off all the CDs and DVDs onto something more permanent. Once images are stored on a solid state device, I would expect them to be more readily available for transfer to whatever new storage media will evolve in the distant future.

Do not rely on storing pictures on a camera memory card – you will want to delete them in the future next time you want to use the card in your camera.

A modern computer can have very large storage capacity built into its hard drive, capable of holding thousands of quality images. While this is convenient and might give you confidence that your images are safe, it is vital that these images are backed up for storage elsewhere, either on DVD as in my case until a few years ago or in something like an external hard drive or high-capacity solid state device. A computer gives little or no notice of when its hard drive is about to fail, and when it does fail the images on it can be lost for all time if not backed up externally, as once happened to my daughter Claire. The minimum should be to ensure that images on your computer are backed up externally before the pictures on the camera's memory card need to be deleted. Or buy a new memory card!

Finding them again

As with photographs on film, digital photographs amass into huge numbers over time, and you do need to have a system that will help you find any one picture quickly. That is not too difficult nowadays because a computer's filing system has a search facility. Also, my camera numbers the individual photographs from 00001 upwards. In some cameras, this counting reverts to zero when you change a memory card. You can teach the camera, in the Settings part of its menu, to keep the previous number sequence going when you change the memory card, so if the last number is DSC01234, for example, the new card will start automatically at DSC01235. When I make a Photoshop image, I change the three prefix letters to a pair that tells me what camera I used. On my computer filing system, I put each group of pictures in dated folders such as '170123 Spain' where the date is rendered YYMMDD so that the computer always presents the folders in date order; wording after the date indicates the subject matter. So long as the individual pictures go in the correct folders, you can find them all easily.

The lesson from this, which took me some years to wake up to, is that you do not need to set up a separate database of digital photographs. The computer filing system can do it for you.

But please do not forget to back them up regularly.

Slide shows

I give many slide shows in a year, all of which are digital. The images I project are from several sources, negatives, slides or digital originals; they can be mixed in one show, as they are in this book. I have seen people put slide shows together on their computer and then be surprised that, when they project them, they appear in a different order from that intended. 'I put them in the right order on the computer,' is a common tale. The fact is that computers always arrange files in alpha/numeric order. If you are using the basic Windows filing system for your show, you will need to prefix each slide's file description with a number or letter that sets the slide in the correct order.

I find it is better to use a programme such as Powerpoint; this is part of the Microsoft Office suite, and is an excellent tool for placing slides in exactly the order you want to display them, as well as giving you the opportunity to add notes, titles, locations and so on. All images to be used as slides should be reduced in size to fit the output size of the projector, usually a width of 1,024 pixels, though modern projectors can project more than this. That indeed is the quality limitation. If the projector cannot resolve an image to anything bigger than 1,024 by 768 pixels, why make big files in the first place? Just make sure you have saved the full-size image file somewhere else so as to maintain its image quality for other purposes such as printing.

Powerpoint can do other useful things. It has a timing facility under the Transitions tab. In this you can set the maximum time each slide should show on the screen. You can set it to change automatically after, say, 60econds, and also on a click of your mouse. This helps me as a discipline. If I waffle on, the computer changes to the next slide, so I know that I will not overrun the time allocated for my slide show. I set the total time to be about 20 per cent longer than the time allocated to me, The slides I move on by clicking the mouse usually shorten the overall time to about that needed by my hosts, so I finish at the required time.

Another feature of Powerpoint that I do not use is the use of a variety of styles of fading between one slide and the next. To me, these fades are a distraction. I prefer a clean change from one projected image to the next, just like a show using physical slides.

This Fuji FinePix 2200 'compact' camera was bundled in with a computer and scanner, and was my first digital camera. While it looks small and neat in the picture, it is actually significantly bigger and heavier than either my Rollei 35 or the Voigtländer folding camera. It produces 2.1 megapixels. A pixel is basically a dot or grain, millions of which make up the image, not totally unlike the grains of silver on black-and-white negatives. 2.1 million pixels is basic, coarse grain; enough to produce an image that will print to A6 or postcard size, or to whole-plate or A5 size if you are lucky. For that to work, the photograph has to be well within the camera's limited capabilities. However, this Fuji camera was good enough to keep in my briefcase for those chance photographs that I might come across on my travels when I did not carry a serious camera with me.

My first digital SLR, which I purchased early in 2004, was a Konica-Minolta A1 that could produce five million pixels. That camera was excellent, and enabled me to stop using films for good. It had a brilliant zoom lens that would stretch from 28mm to 200mm if my memory recalls correctly, so I needed no secondary lenses for this camera. Five million pixels gave me just enough quality to print up to A3 size, so long as one did not look too closely at the print – very good at normal viewing distance. There was a settings wheel at the top which enabled the camera to be set for things such as Auto, Shutter Priority, Aperture Priority, Scenes, Sunsets, and so forth. I left it set on Programme, so that it did what I wanted. Most of the other buttons for its various features, for example White Balance, were on the back and one side. It was too easy to press any of these accidentally when handling the camera, and mistakes could be made, such as inadvertently resetting the white balance, not a good thing if you were under orange street lamps at the time – it is quite a palaver to get the white balance corrected to pure white light if you can't find any! This camera was stolen in Canada in November 2004. Its replacement was the next model, the A2, which is the one in the illustration. This one produces eight million pixels which is sufficient for most well-lighted subjects.

My current camera, which I bought in 2008 after my Konica-Minolta A2 got so wet it stopped working, is this Sony Alpha 200, made after Sony swallowed up Konica. The camera's excellent optics appear to be descended from Minolta; with the benefit of Sony's electronic expertise in image processing, this is my best ever camera. I am reluctant to upgrade from it. At 10.2 million pixels and set at 100ASA, it is equivalent to a very fine grain 35mm camera in its quality of output. The camera has an exposure range from ISO100 to ISO3200. While there is noticeable grain at the largest ISO settings, it enables one to take moving photographs in the light of station lamps, should one want to do so. Its main advantage is that one can, with Photoshop or other image adjustment software, pull out the detail from dark areas such as the wheels and underframes of trains without there being noticeable noise ('grain'). I use this camera with two lenses, the 18mm to 70mm zoom it came with, and one that takes me out to 200mm for reaching longer-distant subjects. These figures are equivalent 35mm camera figures. The actual ones on a digital camera with its smaller image capture frame size are expressed in smaller numbers.

This is my second flatbed scanner and is the one I used to scan the large-format negatives used in the production of this book. It is an Epson Perfection 4900 Photo scanner and can copy papers of up to A4 size. Its negative carrier takes film of 2¼ inches width. I use it at 1,200 dots per inch when scanning negatives, and usually 300 dots per inch when scanning photographic prints. With one exception, none of the images in this book were scanned from prints – all scanned images were from the original negatives or slides.

I just put this picture in to show how much smaller than a 35mm cassette is one of the camera memory cards that fit my DSLRs. My latest memory card which I bought in 2017 can hold sixteen gigabytes of pictures, 125 times the storage capacity of the one in this picture which is one of my first cards. Some cards can store 64GB of pictures, but I do not need all that. Sixteen gigabytes can hold over 3,000 JPEG pictures at my high quality setting. Actually, my wife's Nikon compact camera uses cards that are about one quarter the physical size of my SanDisk cards for the same capacity.

After the failures of two slide and film scanners in ten years, I have purchased this plustek scanner that I have now got used to and which performs well enough to have scanned most of the slides and 35mm negatives used in this book that were taken between 1962 and 2004. I use it with VueScan free software on my computer, which is better than the software supplied with the scanner, and is certainly easier to use. The only one of the three switches on the front of the scanner that I actually use is the on/off switch at the bottom. All other functions are controlled by the scanning software. The scanner has two film feeders, the one for slides which is shown in this photograph, and a similar one that takes a strip of six 35mm negatives.

When I first started printing digitally I used a typical Epson ink-jet printer with Jessops glossy photo paper; I was brought up on glossy, which publishers liked, and old habits die hard. I used to find that, if a print made on that equipment was on display, it would fade significantly over a couple of years or more. I blamed the ink, though that ink actually did not fade if printed on ordinary plain general-user paper. I changed my printer to one that uses pigment inks, and the problem went away. This is the printer in the picture, which is an Epson Stylus Photo R2400 printer that can output up to A3 size. I love it. I also have a Ricoh colour laser printer which produces strong images which are quite acceptable for some purposes, such as producing leaflets, posters, club magazines and so on. An affordable laser printer can never produce the quality one wants for proper photographic images, however.

This is my smartphone. This has taken several photographs that appear in Chapter 8, as well as one or two in the Appendices. It is a Microsoft Lumia 640, based on a former Nokia model upgraded, and cost a fifth of the prices quoted for some of the upmarket phones we keep seeing being recommended on TV or in magazines. The results from its tiny digital camera are, to me, impressive, particularly when I have to take pictures in poor light. The mobile phone's camera's judgement on ISO speed, shutter speed and aperture do really seem to optimise what would be a difficult shot with my DSLR, even if I set the latter to 'Auto' mode. The Lumia 640 camera has another useful feature. If I need to find a serial number on an item of 'white goods' such as a desktop computer or washing machine, and the plate bearing the serial number is behind the item in a relatively inaccessible place, I just poke my mobile phone round the back and photograph the plate. Amazingly the serial numbers are remarkably readable this way, and no heavy lifting or tedious disconnecting is needed. You read it here first!

Recent mobile phone models and smartphones have a duplicate camera lens in the front of the 'phone which enables people to take pictures of themselves, the increasingly popular – and at times really annoying – 'selfie'. This is not something I recommend. I prefer to photograph, say, the Taj Mahal in all its glory without my old face blocking part of the view. However, my wife and I did try one such photograph when we were visiting Santiago de Compostela in northern Spain early in January 2017. We had been drawn to that lovely old city and its cathedral that is the destination aimed at by millions of pilgrims from across Europe. Having seen the cathedral outside and in, we walked out from there towards a park from which, we had been told, there was a good view of the cathedral. Sitting on a bench next to a tree, I aimed the front-facing lens at Mary and me with the cathedral (and its scaffolded tower) in the background. Having composed the view in the phone's screen I could not reach the button without losing the composition, so my wife pressed the button. I am amazed that we and the cathedral have all been rendered reasonably sharp in the image. This raises the question of copyright. As Mary pressed the button, the law says she is the copyright holder. But I held the camera and composed the picture. I think I have to claim joint copyright!

RULES FOR COMPOSITION; CAMERA TECHNIQUES

I may be venturing into the area of 'teaching grandmother to suck eggs' when I suggest a few rules that can be useful for railway photographers, not just how to use a camera but how to lay out the picture that appears in the viewfinder or on the back screen of the camera. These rules are by now largely second nature for me. They come from many sources including art lessons at school, books I have read in the past and comments in photographic portfolios, and they are not by any means solely related to photography of railways. I have selected those, however, that can be helpful in turning a railway scene into a picture. They are not the only rules, I am sure, but they help me. Rules, unlike laws, are made to be broken, but only when the final result would be better than if they were followed slavishly.

By looking through the photographs in this book after reading this Appendix, you should be able to see immediately where I have deviated from the rules I have written, which is very often. In my photography, I have got to the stage where most of my composing of a photograph in the camera is done sub-consciously. People keep telling me at my slide shows that I show good pictures, so I must be doing something right!

Actually, there are not many significant rules, so it is easy to remember the key ones. This Appendix does however try to put some flesh on the bones of the basic rules, and I hope readers find this useful.

Frame the picture

We want the person looking at a photograph to be led to what is the main subject and not be distracted. Looking at a photograph of a train running along a track, it is easy to let the viewer's eye wander off one side of the photograph or the other, particularly if the back of the train is off the edge of the picture. This can be avoided with a little care. By using items in the scene, such as bushes, poles, electrification uprights, trees, or whatever is there, and placing one or other of these

This picture of Austrian Federal Railways Co-Co 1020.43 piloting a Class 1110 Co-Co electric leaving the Arlberg Tunnel at St Anton uses the tunnel mouth as a left frame and back-stop. It matters not that the rest of the train is not visible. The electrification uprights also form a frame at the extreme left of the picture, while the right hand trees act as a frame to the right.

behind the train, and if possible also in front of the train as it will appear in the frame, visual stops can be set up that will prevent the eye wandering off. It is more important to have one at the rear of the train because the natural perspective of receding carriages or wagons tends to draw the eye towards the distant part of the train.

Some frames appear naturally in railways, such as bridges, signal gantries and overhead electrification structures. Or a main station overall roof can be used to focus attention on the train beneath. It is possible also to have a person standing at the point where a frame is needed, and this can be quite effective.

Never off the edge
If you are photographing a train, rather than an individual locomotive, do not cut off the back of the train by the edge of the picture. It is better to have the train rear emerging from a bridge or appearing

from behind a bush. Ideally, you probably want to see the whole train from front to back, but sometimes the site is just not long enough to do that. So use whatever visual stop is there. My 'own goal' in this respect is the picture of the 98-years-old Austrian 0-6-0 in Chapter 2; my excuse is the extreme excitement at the time of seeing such an apparition still working in 1958! At least the curl of smoke coming from the depot frames the train.

Cutting off the back of a train by the edge of the picture usually looks amateurish, believe me.

Intersection of two thirds - or 'not in the middle'
I am repeatedly advising photographers to follow this rule. When framing the image in the camera viewfinder or back screen, the main subject should normally be placed at or near the intersection of two of the thirds. In Figure 1 there are four marked points where this might occur. In

Many amateur photographers do this. They place the main subject bang in the middle of the picture, and let the back of the train run off the edge. Does not it look awful? To achieve this illustrative result, I trimmed off the left of a better-composed picture of a 37 and an 'Ethel' train heat locomotive on the West Highland line, but it makes the point.

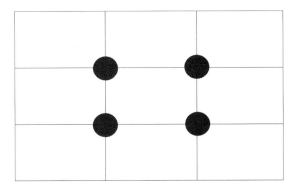

The Intersection of two thirds.

a photograph of a train in the landscape, the centre of interest would normally be placed at the intersection of one or other of the lower two thirds. If the train is on a bridge or embankment, it could be one of the upper thirds.

Many photographers do not think about composition – they usually just place the main subject bang in the middle of the frame every time. If the front of the locomotive is in the middle of the picture, pictorially that usually leaves too much space in front of the train and not enough at the back. So, a train moving from left to right should have its front on or near the right lower intersection, and one moving from right to left should be placed on or near the left lower intersection. As a train is a long thing, I find one often can't do this to the letter, but it is sometimes possible to have the length of the train along the lower third line across the frame, that is between the two lower points in the diagram. The easiest interpretation of this rule is simply to avoid having the centre of interest bang in the middle of the picture if you can.

Many of the pictures in this book fail to obey this rule, I know. There is usually a good reason why they do that, sometimes because pictorial framing gets in the way. But if you do intend to break this rule, know why you are doing it.

When taking colour slides in particular, this rule is important because you cannot easily correct errors afterwards.

Run the track out of a corner

If there is a choice, it is a good practice to place the train in the frame so that the track it is running on leaves the picture at one or other of the bottom corners. This is aesthetically more satisfying and helps to remind the photographer not to have too much or too little stuff in the near foreground. It does depend on the angle of the shot, however. This rule may not always be a natural one to keep and it is not always possible. My picture of the Vivarais train in Chapter 7 illustrates this rule well.

Change the shape of the picture

Not every picture needs to be shaped like a rectangle, neither need it be the same shape as the camera made it. For the sake of this book, most of the photographs in it are rectangular, I know, but there are

This view of a 'Royal Scot' piloting an 'atlantic' on the Stapleford Park miniature railway has the track running out of the bottom left corner of the picture. But what other key composition rule does this image break?

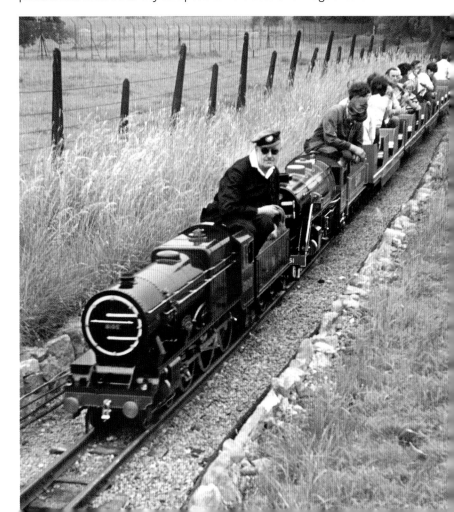

'Letterbox' format suits this record of two Norwegian State Railways General Motors Co-Cos standing at Fauske waiting to cross the Arctic Circle southbound with the day train from Bodø to Trondheim in summer 1973. The sky is featureless, and the foreground plain and dull, so cropping both from the image keeps the eye on the main subject, the locomotives.

exceptions. The picture of the S15 4-6-0 at Grosmont in Chapter 8 is square because that format suited it best and makes it more interesting with unusual impact. Many train-in-landscape pictures are better in 'letterbox' format, long and thin. To fit the page layout in this book, the book designer has skilfully trimmed several pictures from their original shape to nearer 'letter-box'.

Do not ignore the possibility of using vertical format pictures. These often have more impact simply because they are a minority in a book or article. And in a book this size and shape they can show up better by occupying a full page. Seek out those that are vertical in this book, and see for yourself how they impact.

And a few basic rules:
Last but not least there are some basics we should all follow.

Straighten up your pictures. When the camera is not held level, the picture looks odd, particularly if a horizon slopes when it should be level. Hold your camera level and upright if you can. If not, retrim your print so that it is straight, or rotate the image in Photoshop, or whatever else you need to do to bring the final picture up straight.

Keep the camera level. If the camera is level, vertical things like buildings and poles can come out straight up. If the camera is pointing upwards or downwards a bit, vertical things in the picture will not be vertical. Buildings will have a vertical perspective, and poles will lean, even if they were not leaning in real life. Correcting perspective distortion can be done in Photoshop or a similar software, but it is better not to have to do it if the camera can be held level. I find the frequent leaning buildings in television news reports very annoying; do not copy them!

Focus where you want the picture to be sharp. If your camera uses auto-focus, make sure you know where it is focusing before you press the shutter release, and if necessary move the focus point to where you want it to be.

Set the shutter speed appropriately. For a fast moving train, nothing less than 1/1000th second exposure will normally work to keep the front of the train sharp. For still pictures, use at least 1/100th if there is enough light. It is surprising how even a little camera movement can render an image less than pin-sharp.

LIFE AFTER DEATH

This may sound a bit morbid. The theme of this Appendix exists on the assumption that every railway photographer would like to see his or her collection kept for posterity and if possible used for the wider benefit after the photographer's death. I, for one, do not want my negatives, slides and digital images to end up in a skip. So, we have to face up to the future in a positive way.

It is worth thinking about this now. Not all of us will live to a ripe old age. Sadly, even young people fall victim to disease or fatal accidents, and such things appear to be quite random however low the probability may seem that it will be our turn next.

So, I hear you say, what have I done about it? Am I practicing what I preach? Well, yes. I have written my will, and in it I have bequeathed my photographic collection to a trust that will look after it.

There are really only a few ways of ensuring the continuation of one's collection. These include:

- Keeping it in the family
- Giving it to a friend
- Giving or selling it to an established body that will use it in the future

Keep it in the family
If the photographer has family, sons or daughters or other young people with an interest in railway photography and the knowledge of how to make use of the collection, then by all means make sure you have made it clear who gets your collection and what you want to happen to it. The important thing is that that person actually wants to take it over. Despite all the best intentions of people near and dear to you, dropping a huge pile of slides and negatives onto a grieving spouse or partner who is clearing out your stuff could be just one more burden that that hapless person has to bear, and the lot could still be thrown out with the rubbish as being the easiest way to clear it.

So, write your vision for your collection into your will, after making sure the intended recipient is happy about you doing that.

Give it to a friend
This has to be someone with like interests to yours, who actually wants you to do this and who has the time and inclination to do what you want that person to do with the collection. Again, it is sensible to put it into your will.

Pass it to a trust or other body
Many of us use our photographic collections publicly by submitting them for publication. The historical nature of some collections, like the earlier decades of mine, may make them attractive to bodies such as Colour-Rail, the Transport Trust and similar businesses; these are set up to exploit photographs in books and magazines, possibly with greater energy and success than the photographer managed in his or her own lifetime. Bodies like these usually have a legal existence that makes it certain that the collections are held together for posterity.

There are two things you can do with this idea. You can find a body who will buy your collection now; some do advertise in magazines. Or you can arrange with the body to accept your collection at a later date or when you die. In either case, having got the body's consent to your plan it is best to put it in your will so that there is legal pressure to get the handover right. That is what I have done.

I know of some photographers who moved their collections into trusts or other bodies about the time when managing the photographs themselves was becoming difficult as old age rendered them less capable. They were still able to receive reproduction fees from their pictures because of the arrangement they had made with the body that was managing them on their behalf. So they had the pleasure of seeing their stuff appearing in print, and of being paid, without the hassle of submitting the photographs to publishers themselves.

If you have lots of pictures of foreign, that is not British, railways, the choice of recipients is more limited. My collection is currently bequeathed to a trust that already handles at least one collection that is very much a source of world-wide photographs of railways. Each body has its own area of interest, so check it out before making your final decision.

Catalogue

Just make sure the recipient has the means of finding photographs when he or she has your collection. A catalogue or listing is always helpful. Very few will have the time to make a catalogue themselves, and they may not have the knowledge to identify trains, locations or dates properly. So, find time to summarise where each group of your pictures sits, even if you can't list them all.

One task I have set myself is to disentangle family and other pictures from railway ones in my collection. Hopefully, you may already have done this.

POSTSCRIPT

'The world is a book and those who do not travel read only one page.'

Saint Augustine (born Thagaste 354AD; educated Carthage)